WINNERS!

WILLIAM BOYE

WINNERS!

RISING FROM THE FOOT
OF THE WOMEN'S
FOOTBALL PYRAMID

CONTENTS

CONTENTS

THE INAUGURATION

This narrative began in the Spring of 2015 when a friendly against Viking FK Ladies sparked a communal belief that Ashford Town (Middlesex) FC should establish a female side, a successful one at that.

Having departed Middlesex FA Girls' Centre of Excellence where two congenial seasons with the under 17's, was followed up with a swotting Coach Mentor; this manufactured an obsessive, determined and pretentious football coach in me. By virtue of, and unashamed to admit, I possess an unimaginable desire to impress and succeed. Thwacked into me as a youth at Bishop Bowers Catholic Archdiocese of Accra. A strict private school located in the capital of Ghana stowed the very foundations that The Tangerines were modelled on. Knowledge, love and service.

Gunnersbury Catholic School was the all boys secondary school that welcomed me to England but it was not until I went to their successful sixth form that women's football became an improbable passion. I arranged a charity football match for the sixth form women to host against Gumley House, the sister school of a small cohort of faith schools in the borough. A resounding defeat, which we'll gloss straight over, was met with a mammoth crowd that swarmed me with pride. As a young man this was a rare emotion but one I enjoyed the feeling of.

Frankly, it is easy to see how this vortex of a journey began; yearning for something of my own. Obsessed with becoming knowledge rich, to love the individuals that placed their trust in me and devoted in providing long-term service to this project; I possessed a burning desire to take this undiscovered football club right to the very top.

PRELUDE

To start a football club from scratch is not for the faint-hearted. It is a journey that features desolation, pain, joy, excitement and happiness. One day there is an implicit wave of expectation to succeed, this is very quickly met with a purposeful craving to see you decline.

The blueprint was not a short-term project, it simply could not be. Being emptied into the foot of the pyramid; quelled, suppressed and stifled, this was a long-term expedition being assembled. Erratically illustrated were names of modern football clubs; what they looked like, how they operated, what structure they had in place. This very quickly allowed the foundations to be solidified, bit by bit.

Yes frustration, disappointment and failure is the emotion discerned when four managers in four years scuttle through the revolving door of a reserve team that deserve so much more.

Consistent success does not happen overnight. To have achieved four league titles, four back to back promotions, two of the most successful FA Cup runs the club has ever endured and a total of ten trophies for the senior first team is something I cannot wait for you to read about.

A SPECIAL NOTE

This book primarily focuses on the initial seven years I experienced at Ashford Town (Middlesex) FC Women; it's a narrative on the growth of the club and details on our rise to what many define as success.

Highly delicate conversations and intimate details of what takes place inside the football club is unfortunately for most, where it will remain, behind closed doors. Regrettably this is not a gossip column but a book that reflects ideas, opinions and key events that have led to the wonderful accomplishments of grassroots players and coaches, unheard of at the elite level, until now.

This in turn, should elucidate how and why we rose from the foot of the women's football pyramid, to the dizzy heights of the FA Women's National League.

TRUDGING INTO THE BOARDROOM

Driving into the car park was enthralling; being jilted side to side by stone crafted speed bumps was quickly converged with a pot hole that my VW seemed all too pleased to feel. The drive up to the boardroom seemed like forever. With my nose singed in petrichor, to the left of me was a grass field transitioned into parking bays, and an isolated turnstile that lay dormant for centuries. To my right were a number of youth pitches in pristine condition; although one was representative of grassroots from the distant past. A mud pit that was a Cruyff-turn away from a dislocated ankle, hosting a first team that seemed intimately savvy with the conditions they were training on. I slowed down to absorb it all, unbeknown to my cognizant psyche plotting just how this would all work out. Eventually, I park up and spot the meeting space. A bright blue porta cabin was home to board members who compressed themselves around the room and installed themselves into their chairs that instantly erected their vertebrae to prove they meant business. A deafening silence broke as just how to initiate this meeting was lost until the late chairman, Dave Baker, a man held in such prestigious regard, fragmented it by welcoming the three representatives which included me, my eventual centre forward and prospective captain, Bear.

An assiduous woman with so much heart and passion for the game, she worked doggedly to have me return to our previous victory haven before this meeting was logged into the diary. The club meant so much to me, I worked there on work-experience and gained coach-experience in their bygone centre of excellence. To be frank and candid, I saw it as my break in becoming a professional manager that would go on to manager his motherland Ghana. The joy of youth ey! But managing the women's was a great experience - we achieved so much success, it seemed such a waist to leave it all behind. But the Bees were adamant we were not to return and Bear just loved playing the game too much to leave it all behind. I loved that football club, we both did, but for the door to rammed shut in our faces despite the opposite being promised, simply left a pungent taste in the mouth. As the power that be has it, you're never down on your luck for too long; unbeknown to me, I was sat ogling at the future.

Rumours had circulated that Ashford were open to a woman's team as they were originally home to one, quite some years prior. Not one to boast about, so I'm told; like a dirty secret never to be yanked out of the memory bank. So this needed to be an enhancement and quite frankly the potential was there. This was a ground famous for hosting cup finals, which we knew all too well. So the infrastructure was there. Anyone involved with grassroots football recognize the challenges associated with starting from scratch and uncovering a spot to call home. This was not even something our previous club, well established in the women's football pyramid even held. Years of competing and still no digs. Still no identity. Still no progression. Eventually, the players felt it. This is ultimately, why I found myself in the cerulean trailer concocting this new challenge. Along with the fact I was spurned. It hurt, and maybe I found myself sat in these new surroundings because subconsciously I craved revenge. Either way, a change was brewing.

The panel begun with a speech on how a *ladies* team once represented the famous tangerines, but their behaviour in the clubhouse and habits simply did not manifest what they desired. This somewhat pleased me, it conveyed a shared message - standards. The board members were serious about their football club, they were passionate about everything Ashford and wanted the future to be brighter than their stripes. Though accepting of their derelict past, there was an eagerness to evolve and succeed. This was music to my ears. Although as they continued, my facials changed.

'So you have in place your code of conduct, club constitution, committee and players right?'

The blood drained from my mug as these outlandish questions continued. We clearly had not prepared. We thought this would be easy to start but obviously did not do our homework on just what needed to be in place and submitted for this deranged decision to be approved by all parties. Bear and I exchanged a befuddled glance.

'Nothing has been setup yet but we'll get there' I acknowledged.

'There's a lot of time before the start of the new season but try to get all of this into Middlesex FA when you can' they countered.

'I will get straight onto it.' But just after this response of mine, the subject shifted pretty quickly...

'It's important to also stress that despite being affiliated, financially we will operate separately' the vice-chair instructed.

'Uh huh, no problem, I totally understand'.

I really didn't, but I was so pleased that this was actually going ahead, I was happy to just get out of there. I knew my previous club charged membership fees to players but I never really comprehended what this went towards - I would soon enough come to realize just how costly it all was to run a football club. Not quite the dream it's sold as if you're not willing to invest as a chairman and pull in the sponsors you need to operate. At this stage, I had just completed my UEFA B Coaching License, I *loved* learning, I embraced the process of being stressed as a problem-solver, determined to find my way through anything and everything. My brain was like a sponge, it just loved soaking up new information so to learn how to setup, operate and run a football club was something I secretly enjoyed the process of because working in sales at the time I identified so many correlations between the two. Goals, KPI's, pitching, selling, I could go on but fortunately I got to use my existing knowledge and skills to get this off the ground.

I paced into the boardroom as a football coach, and left as the chairman and manager of Ashford Town (Middlesex) FC Women. Within weeks my phone was roaring; players were peering for new opportunities, whilst others were simply desperate for a way out. This report had spread so fast, it proved just how small of a circle football was, women's football in particular.

Tittle-tattle had reached me that players were looking for an out, at my previous club. *Shock.* To my dissatisfaction I couldn't bring players along, the season was not completed, but I could hold open training for prospective new players to join. Let me tell you now if someone had told me that players would drop down four divisions to play for me I would tell you, of course and pigs might fly. But boy did this open training session open my eyes.

It schooled me on just how important players are to a club. How important it is to respect the individuals at your football club; how to treat them; how not to treat them; how important it is to listen to what they want as well as what they need. A lesson I assimilated very early on this adventure. It is integral that players are at the heart of the decisions you make... conclusively, *this* is the recipe for success.

Winning the County Cup with Brentford FC Women in the 2013/
14 football season, defeating QPR.
Brentford WFC

Winning! During my time at Brentford Women's we lifted five trophies in two seasons.
Brentford WFC

Brentford FC Assistant Manager, Alan Kernaghan, joined me in
a training practice in 2013.
Brentford WFC

COMPOSING A BLUEPRINT

Drawing up this blueprint was my only desire, strutting out of that azure cabin. I was itching to get going. I needed a plan to ensure everything discussed in the boardroom wasn't just rubbish, in fact I was going to standby my promise to the board members and players.

I begun highlighting modern-day clubs that boasted sturdy foundations and a bright future. Clubs from tiers one to four, where we aspired to be. It was also football, netball and hockey clubs that I had paid specific attention to because these sports had seen a prodigious rise in participation and the clubs in which a laser focus was administered enjoyed commendable longevity, a sustainable future, an infectious training and match day environment, and a player-centred approach that led to success on and off the turf.

I was fortunate enough to also be supported by an Ashford Town representative in Gareth Coates - an ever so helpful friend who nothing was ever too much trouble for. He provided me with with what I needed to get this essentially passed by our respective county football association. I was finally there and had drawn up action points to complete; this constitution was built and concluded in a week and consisted of:

- The name the club will be formally go by.
- Association(s) the club will be affiliated to and bound by their rules.
- Organization(s) conformed in supporting the club.
- Objectives of the club.
- How membership will be conducted as a self-financing entity.
- Devoted individuals to be voted secretary, treasurer and welfare officer.
- Powers of the committee.
- How annual general meetings will be conducted.
- Special general meetings; when and how they will be conducted.
- Protection policies that aligns with the FA's safeguarding handbook.

- Exceptional practice that everyone will adhere to.
- Individualized code of conduct for players, coaches and spectators.
- Disciplinary procedures.

Once I turn my head to something, I am pretty determined to see it through, not much can deter me from it. I would wake up and write, sit in the canteen on my lunch break and write, arrive home and write! Yes, I wanted it finished it was hardly the most enthralling part of engendering this football team. But, I felt genuinely invested in every minuscule bit of this club I was forming. It was like my little baby, so it's no surprise I treated every bit of this part with love, care and devotion. Maybe to some it felt like an unhealthy obsession, but I envisaged an incomparable anecdote unearthing.

I returned to the boardroom this time to hand over this weighty document and to formally agree to begin the football club, Monday 23rd February 2015. This was the beginning.

In order to make this work I would need to pioneer a philosophy, a DNA, a blueprint...and it was this fifty-page-document, this handbook, that guided us to success. It was composed to assist the personnel within the small circle of the football club in understanding the expectations when sporting the crest. It also acted as a reference throughout the football season for coach development.

I looked at how the new generation of coaches viewed coaching and quite simply wanted different for my group of players. If we were to work through the divisions to reach the Women's National League, then I needed devotion and for the coach to feel that sense of long-term responsibility to the cause. Not all, but many of the modern-day coaches we see today view the role as digressive and short term; never planning on committing to a club. So I composed a development plan to support coaches at the club and as a result I would receive their long-term committal. And I meant indestructible commitment and constancy; what it used to mean when Football Italia and Renford Rejects were aired in the early noughties and not what the world has transitioned it to today. Coach development was an important part of this blueprint, because of the convolution around coaching. The coach has to possess many skills like communication, planning, networking, reflection, as well as developing knowledge in a number of areas like pedagogy. But in our early stages at the club, I recognized that the coach needed to be open to a dual role, which could include being an assistant, and completing a range of admin tasks, away from the grass. I felt that the ability to manage all of these roles successfully would assemble an effective coaching programme with learning and development a constant driver.

The goal as chairman and manager was to create a winning senior culture whilst allowing for players to develop and fulfil their potential in a patient, fun, enjoyable, positive yet highly challenging environment. Within this goal it was imperative every team would work in correspondence with each other by playing football in an identical style.

This is arguably where things went wrong for the 'B' Team. This document was always a guide to success and never gospel. There was a drive to play football in an identical style to the first team so that when players were promoted to play up, they would be accustomed to the tactics, formations and strategies adopted. However, there needed to be an appreciation for contrasting approaches to the game because different oppositions pose contrastive threats. It should never have been a one-size-fits-all approach and this is ultimately why the first team were able to adapt, progress and achieve promotion after promotion whilst the 'B' team saw a change in manager every year and steered into the opposite direction.

The name for our 'B' Team derived from the decision that this was a second senior team to our first team women. They were not a youth development team nor were they full of experience not quite ready for first team action, they were very much a mix of individuals at different stages of their football journey. So the same needed to be reflective of this. Their head coach also needed to be homogeneous. Again and again, modern-day coaches are entering the grassroots game with very little knowledge of the expectations that will be placed upon them, in both the coaching environment and their coaching development. You can manage their expectations as much as possible by declaring this in the interview process, but this is not entirely understood until they take on the job.

The B Team's first coach applied for the role, told me what I wanted to hear from a young and hungry coach and just like that he was in the door. A disappointing appointment and a mistake I still rue today. He possessed phenomenal footballers with untold amounts of potential. The vast majority arrived from Teddington Athletic that contained a top-tier youth setup. I know this first hand as they were a club I quondamly mentored during my time with The FA, along with Southall, Staines Lammas, and NPL Youth. They had dedicated coaches who valued the women's game, including coaches who valued their education. These players who transferred over to our B Team had a two-year window because they were destined for university; I'm talking brains as well as the ability on the turf. They played some mesmerizing football at times but quite literally lacked any sort of direction. I would often pick up their manager and give him a lift to and from training but he would miss the odd game because he had plans. These plans became more frequent and just as I begun to lose patience with his recurring absenteeism, so did the players. He was away that often, when we made the decision to cut ties, as a multidisciplinary team, his disappearance was not even felt by the players.

The succeeding coaches came with so much hope and excitement because they contrastingly committed a lot, *in the beginning*. They both guided as joints managers in the same division as our senior first team, so I felt they were an absolute steal. This was an opportunity, I felt, for players to increase performance and bridge the ability gap that existed within the two senior sides.

Their first practice did not disappoint either, one of the very few times an offensive phase of play was designed and delivered at their level. You couldn't wipe the grin off my face. The players were finally designed a practice that exposed them to similar pictures to what they encountered on Sunday's. As you can guess the results greatly improved, morale was at an all-time high, the football on show was good but yet again... this was short lived. They just stopped turning up to training and stopped communicating. They knew if they were not present, the first team coaches would step up and deliver, so to them there were no repercussions for their absences. As before, the writing was on the wall, and eventually a replacement was in.

Time to move on. This new appointment was a good character, a genuine attentive coach, I felt we had a good one for the long-term, as the team now needed that continuity. He was such a skilled coach, predominantly with the younger players as his skill set lay in youth coaching. Again, the delivery of practices were good, but this time I felt this coach lacked the sufficient subject content knowledge to teach practices past a basic level. As a result, the participants did not feel as though they were being challenged and begun questioning, and rightly so, their progression. I signed players' to the B Team on the basis that they would get first team experience, but they were just no where near the level required for first team football. It's no wonder they would feel frustrated at the repetition of similar basic sessions, lose on the weekend and wrangle amongst themselves. This proceeded for quite some time and eventually had a considerable impact on the commitment and motivation of all participants, and I mean both players and coach. Their head coach stepped down, having told me in training, in the middle of a session...

'Oh just so you're aware, the end of the month will be my last session,' he declared.

'No worries, thank you for letting me know', I quickly responded. There were no decorous designations from me, only effectively delivering the practices the players deserved. Some part of me feels he wanted me to entreat, in the hope he will reverse his decision. Maybe he never felt valued, maybe he never felt supported who knows, but to my disappointment, another one bites the dust. This one did hurt, because I offered him the opportunity to be mentored, to observe his practices and feedback - he point-blank refused and he didn't want to feel... *watched.* I give you the small proportion of modern-day coaches and their view to learning and development. The modern-day coaches I always appear to stumble on. Maybe it was the blueprint that needed tweaking.

The youth teams in this narrative were also a fiasco of a tale for slightly different reasons. They were at a development stage of their personal development, so it was important everyone embraced the approach all coaches and members of the management shared which was 'we are not and will not accept a win at all costs approach.' I pioneered this purely because I felt it was important to recognize and understand that part of the learning process is to allow young students of the game to explore and take risks in all positions of the pitch without the pressure of doing things "the traditional way", in other words, embracing wrong through developing independent thinkers and excellent decision makers of the game with creativity as well as an unorthodox approach to playing football. Winning football matches are ideal and sometimes it shows progression is taking place however winning or losing is not a way to solely measure player development. Win, lose, or draw, be positive and consistently encourage players.

But with the lack of coaching support and recognizing how challenging recruitment of the right coach is, I tried to do it all. I would coach the first team on a Monday, play myself on a Tuesday, coach the youth on a Wednesday, train with my non-league side on a Thursday, coach another youth team on a Friday, play youth matches on a Saturday morning, play competitively myself on Saturday afternoon, before coaching the senior first team on Sunday... oh yeah, and back to work on Monday morning. You can see exactly where this lifestyle sent me. Single. Then some felt it was to an early grave next, after I hard a cardiac episode at the training ground.

My body had felt the effects of doing more than I should have and eventually I fell to the ground having a seizure right in front of the coaches and player. The warning signs were there I must admit. Dizzy spells, heaviness in the chest, random juddering events, I felt them all. I woke up in the ambulance not knowing where I was or what had happened. The helpful paramedics soon filled me in and I can assure you I have never been more embarrassed. For anyone to be seen in such a weak and vulnerable state is horrible; I felt that and dreaded seeing everyone again. The players were so nice and just wanted to make sure I was okay but all I could playback internally was a help-less image of a lifeless man, out for the count. Enough was enough and in the end I needed to consider my health.

Sooner rather than later players begun dwindling away and joining other, better run, youth setups. As I was being stretched from one team to another I couldn't provide the quality coaching that was expected. I don't just mean de-livery of a practice but the whole process of coaching at grassroots level.

- Being the coach;
- the designated driver;
- orchestrator of lifts and drop-offs;
- match physio;
- kit distributor;
- fixture and results secretary;
- the administrator;
- funding finder;
- the grounds-man on match day having to setup the pitch;
- the ball-boy ploughing through stinging nettles to claw back the footballs.

I am quietly positive there are more, but these are the roles that spring to mind. On top of these duties I found it challenging delivering good quality training practices, that I pride myself on effectively delivering - that ticked these boxes that the blueprint advised:

- Use a positive and enthusiastic manner at all times.
- Include elements of transition in all practices, wherever possible.
- Deliver realistic and game related practices.
- Use an approach that maximizes playing time for all players.
- Use various coaching styles based on the needs of the individual.
- Design practices that enable players to make lots of decisions.

- Ensure learning is player-centred through active involvement.
- Include elements of conditioning, to develop athletic female growth.

All of this needed to happen before even the reflection process took place, where I had to consider what went well, what didn't go so well and ultimately what changes I would make next time round, when delivering. So much needed to happen that I simply abandoned because I was being pulled from pillar to post; I felt as though I was carrying the weight of the world on my shoulders. I took on far too much responsibility that eventually I engendered the opposite effect I wanted to generate. Parents became frustrated and some began yawping what exactly their yearly fees were going towards. Before I could even counter - the number of youth teams reduced significantly. The one pleasing outcome from all of this is that the young players continue to play football elsewhere - for all of the frustration suffered from both parties, this at least shows some success, in fostering a love of the game that means they continue to be involved in the sport, no matter the capacity.

EVENTUALLY IN THE DUGOUT

So, the take-home message in the blueprint is to start embracing wrong; as for much more of our lives wrong is what we usually are. Wrong is how development takes place, wrong is how we learn. So when your athletes are wrong simply:

- Open your mind to different perspectives.
- Be as humanly supportive, whilst imbedding challenge.
- Drive a passionate learning-focused environment.

These three pillars will underpin how you grow the environment you are in because it is not the coach that controls this environment. In fact learning is impacted in every single moment of everyday life, influenced by the people who co-exist in those environments. It is impossible to separate the things that are important to us from the way we think about the players and see the game of football, we are all creatures of habit so be open to alternative perspectives. I went from thinking this to putting it into practice from Monday 30th March 2015 when I was eventually hemmed into the dugout.

'Will, we have an opportunity for a friendly against an overseas team' the vice-chairman proposed.

'That's great, get the game on, it'll be good' I uttered nervously.

It was that neutral feeling of excitement and apprehension. I knew that moment would pass but gazing over to the A3 folio opposite my bed, attached to my magnolia decorated wall, unashamedly with sellotape, was the constant reminder of the cosmic duty that awaited me. Scrawled on, were names of players who would join me in this quest to the Women's National League. Nine names were all I could muster, but I'd soon come to realize just how integral the positive relationships fashioned at my previous clubs, would come to be.

That ubiquitous moment had arrived, a managerial debut that felt like forever was here, this of course is where all of the fun begins. Sat in the dugout gazing over a football pitch that was going to be home; all you could think about were the sheer size of the turf and just how much of a progression this was from an abandoned marsh. Imagine, an actual stadium with north facing seated stands, just imagine this being entirely filled with chanting spectators, this is luxury and this one time pipe-dream was launching. The potential for the women's game was colossal, the opportunity that eyeballed me was stimulating and the players sensed this too.

Players that played under me as manager of Brentford Women were looking for a way out. We enjoyed a successful spell engineering back to back promotions and lifting four trophies in two seasons. Exceptional footballers were at the club, who could play levels above step five of the football pyramid. Picture that; footballers in the peak of their career, albeit at a marsh, playing at tier five, willingly choose to drop down to tier nine, the very bottom of the pyramid. This plight from my previous club was a result of awry judgement, where players were not at the forefront of their thinking and decision-making. I sold the players my objective, I was a salesman by trade at this stage so I was simply doing my job. It paid off for some but not many. The change was too much for some in which their personal allegiance was with the chair and CEO than the club itself.

That sort of attachment is hard to splinter. But the others who felt disregarded took the leap of faith.

Vicky James, Laura Huse, Lavana Neufville, Claire Samuels, Ashley Cheatley and Amber Luzar were the first team players that had decided to move on. On top of this, two from the youth team I spent my illustrious learning years with also joined; Beth Sheehan and Tyra Mills as they turned sixteen years of age, equipped for the step up. They justified the positive effect authentic relationships have in the game with players and parents alike. This was to be my biggest advantage as the narrative progresses but for now, back into the dugout as Viking FK Ladies await.

The word had spread about this friendly fixture so friends had tagged along with the players to make up a ten-strong army before Viking rented us their goalkeeper who was by some stretch, the best player on the pitch. Having a top class number one is a game changer in the game. There are so few in the game, finding one of real quality is such a rarity. I digress.

I paced into the home changing room as the narrow unkept walkway directed me, stepping into the numbing surroundings where the hairs on my arms stood up. Partial nerves, and partially illustrating what chilly an evening greeted us. The pale walls were blemished with desiccated mud and stud marks but it is what lay on the seated benches that unlatched my eyes. Truly a sign of the times... fourteen decrepit tangerine and white stripped long-sleeved tops we were to brandish under the lights, all mens-XL. Matched with carrot coloured socks and all white silk Chelsea FC shorts for fine measure. Frankly, it was ghastly but the fact the players wore it with no fuss said more about their character than maybe mine, at the time. For me, everything had to be perfect, my brain simply explodes if not, but for these inspiring athletes, they just wanted to play the game. Baggy tops, oversized shorts and contrasting socks weren't going to stop them playing under at The Robert Parker Stadium.

The first half was a close affair as we came in drawing 1-1 but the turnout from spectators left the players buoyed, so despite Viking being the better side and deserving at the very least a draw, we won the game. The ferocious machine at the spearhead of our attack notched a brace. With twenty minutes remaining, our Norwegian travelers twice rattled the crossbar and once saw an effort rebound off the post. How we held on to win it, I'll never know, but we did and this grit and tenacity is certainly what underpinned our very future.

The side from the city Stavanger were sporting; Truls Dishington, the team leader, was gracious in defeat and inspired the acceleration of this steam train, I had no ambition in slowing down when we shook hands and spoke at the end.

'Thanks for a great game and wonderful arrangement, something to remember for all of us. It was a perfect match for us to end our training camp!'

'You're too kind, I wouldn't say perfect' I cackled back.

'Honestly, you gave us different type of problems, which is just what we needed' Truls insisted while praising two players in particular who stood out like a sore thumb.

Standing in that dugout was enthralling but boy was it lonely, it didn't help that we were without a single sub...I needed help.

Four months remained, until pre-season got underway so it was the perfect time to put the building blocks in place. As the head, it was instrumental I got things right and made appointments that would continue to ensure a memorable visit to Ashford. This meant I needed to assemble a squad for the long term, that included marquee signings to be the protagonists of this narrative and construct a training programme that inspired industrious workers in which a winning philosophy could be injected into each individual. Time to bring in Matthew Aumeeruddy.

Working for the the FA at the time meant learning and development was what I needed to preach but also adhere to. At the time, The FA were tasked with improving football at the elite level, but recognized it needed a big drive at grassroots level to widen the talent pool for the elite Premier League football clubs to work with. The hope was that this would fashion a domino effect - meaning our national team will have better quality players at their disposal to challenge on the world stage. There was an understanding that this success was not to be achieved overnight and that this would take time; this success was to be underpinned by a philosophy and developmental programme for grassroots players. My role was to deliver this vision to coaches at clubs that I mentored so naturally I adopted this model to support my very own players in their development to enable them to be successful - all documented in my blueprint.

Alongside player characteristics, I outlined a playing approach, or what was branded as 'their DNA', that contained elements for 'in possession' and for 'out of possession'. This model guided my coaching programme as I engrossed these playing elements within both sessions and game experiences to support players in learning the game. Any coach that I was to work with also needed to engage and believe in this model. They needed to be a student of the game and understand every aspect of it. As well a that, I needed a coach I could trust to push and challenge me as well as the players. I needed them to have similarly high expectations, standards and passion for the game... my search was on.

I found myself attending a range of UEFA B coaching courses to simply network and observe how it was run;

maybe it'd provide me with some innovative approaches of my own to take back, I thought. I wanted to see first-hand from senior educational representatives and also to learn if much had changed from when I took my UEFA B coaching course, three years prior. Not much had developed but it did provide me with reassurance that I needed in myself - that I was doing okay. Before leaving I was instantaneously cornered by one of the coaches on the course. Before even introducing himself, he asked

'Who do you work for?'

'I work for The FA, I was coaching at Middlesex Centre of Excellence last year so just came to observe this course today, that's all' I responded.

'How have you found it?' He proceeds abruptly,

'It's good, not much has changed from when I did my UEFA B, bu...'

'Ahh, you've got your UEFA B? He interrupts,

'Yeh I do, and I'm more than happy to help you with yours, if you like? I'm starting my own women's team so there will plenty of opportunities to coach and practice'

'That sounds great', he stuttered, 'how can I get in touch?'

I proceeded by giving him my FA email and concluded the brief exchange; 'get in touch whenever, and I can arrange to get you coaching'.

There was no stopping Matthew, this was the inauguration I would come to realize was not his disability but his ability to push for success. He had emailed the very next day asking for dates for pre-season training, I parked the email as chairmanship had taken a front seat, meetings after meetings, including trying to push for a placement in the higher divisions... and then another email followed a few days later, and another proceeded this.

'Wow, this guy just doesn't stop', I uttered to myself as I sat deliberating; so then I responded inviting him to our practice. I find it very hard to complement myself, it's not something I'm in the habit of doing, but boy am I a genius for adding the mastermind of this operation to the team. I am not too proud to admit that without Matthew this club would not be what it is. What was once a lonely dugout, is now filled with knowledge, direction and mastery.

The Robert Parker Stadium. The inviolable turf.
ATMFC

Early days in the dugout with the mastermind, Matthew
Aumeeruddy
ATMWFC

CHAPTER

4

THE FEROCIOUS MACHINE

Two hundred and forty four goals in one hundred and twenty five appearances...boy did she tick each and every single one of those boxes in the player characteristics blueprint - and then some.

As a sixteen year old, she contained speed, and intelligence, as an eighteen-year-old, she very quickly combined these attributes and established a ravenous eye for goal. In no way is this component a narcissistically composed account of my educational genius to create this machine, but merely a segment that documents her success and how integral it is in understanding the individual, in order to construct a platform for them to be the protagonist of their tale.

Preceding the Viking FK tie, this robot had notched five league goals all season, in seventeen appearances. Without mischievously ravaging your fun, lets contextualize just what this statistic illustrates.

Season	App	Goals
2016/17	15	40
2017/18	24	51
2018/19	27	63
2019/20	17	25
2020/21	13	18
2021/22	29	41
Total	*125*	*244*

A predatory goal scorer right? I knocked on her front door, as she was only local to my parent's quarters.

'Hello Will, come in' her mother enthusiastically exclaimed, as I walked in, leisurely removing my trainers at the front door. Nowadays, I go by the name of Willie to Cheatley's mother Lisa, and her grandma, even to Leah, her sister but not quite to Paul...not just yet anyway. A sign of the tight bond that has been generated over the years.

'How on earth am I going to convince her?' I mumbled nervously to myself. My palms were sweaty and my forehead began to resemble this as I frantically wiped it off in the hallway, still trying to take off these bloody trainers. They new why I was round so there was no need for an introduction, although I couldn't help but think this was an impossible task. To leave a named football club and join a foreign entity with no guarantees of success, just a coach who is parched for success, is just not happening, but here I was shooting my shot.

'I have worked at the elite level Ash and I just know where we can take this...with the players we have I can take this club to the National League, it's where we all want to be right?'

The look on her face was of pure excitement. Maybe that was because my parting decree was along the lines of 'I have applied for us to join the London and South East Regionals, I've submitted the quality of player(s) we'll possess, as they asked for this' we're now just waiting their decision. For me this is what swayed it, that ambition I possessed she saw in herself - she wanted to take the football club to the very top.

All the formalities were concluded and it was time to get back to business. Special players come once in a while, but players of this quality are a rare bread - it must be why my body felt the need to regulate its temperature at that particular moment. She possesses the ability on the pitch where she can create goal-scoring opportunities from absolutely nothing. The audacity of her in and around the eighteen yard box encompasses anything I've seen at this level of the game. Coupled with this is her humbleness - she's completely oblivious to the talent she has. She is always greatly dissatisfied with herself after games, even games she's performed exceedingly well in. She would remember only the things that didn't go well, but that as we all know is often a sign of the person and the player.

Some people often ask me; how have you kept hold of such a forward for so long? how does she record these numbers year after year? what is she doing at Ashford? Well the simple answer to all of those questions is that, she is a winner. As a club we have always been successful in winning league titles and cup competitions, and quite frankly she is addicted to winning. Not because of the sheer number of trophies she's been collecting but because it's a sign that this football club is efficiently accelerating. Who wouldn't want to progress with the club they've achieved so much with? This artist is such a big game player. The amount of outstanding technicians at the football club is untold, a lot better than Cheatley, who pose teams an array of challenges. But they focus on this prolific goal scorer, player mark her, often with two marking her at the same time - and she absolutely thrives off it.

In 2022 we progressed to the final of the county cup, branded Capital Women's Cup, where we were up against Dulwich Hamlet. Having won the junior section when were in division two and the Intermediate section when we were in the Greater London Women's Football League Premier division, we were determined to lift the senior cup too. The final was at Surrey FA's headquarters, the home of Dorking Wanderers, whilst it was an easy enough journey for me from school, others arrived thirty minutes after the meet time, pushing back the time Callum O'Connell could deliver the pre-match analysis, and further repelling players getting their ankles strapped. You can just imagine how wacky my brain was going. Either way, this ferocious machine had to take on board information from the analysis, get her ankled strapped, which had been bothering her from our game 48-hours prior. Yes you heard that right, we had to play this final forty-eight hours after a league fixture whilst our opposition had a two-week rest - make of that what you will. So she came out to warm up with only seven minutes left until we had to return back into the changing rooms. My frustration brewed but of course I tried to contain this, her personality simply does not accept shouting, swearing, or scathing, she's just not that person. In actual fact, neither am I. She needs to be constantly encouraged and feel close to her coach, there needs to be that relationship of unwavering trust because whilst she appreciates honesty, she most certainly is one who needs a gentle approach, so I kept my emotions in check and encouraged the entire group to bring this trophy home. It's arguably the worst I've seen us play - in possession we struggled to sustain possession for large periods, out of possession, we were simply not aggressive enough in regaining the ball, yet we were the team that had created the better chances. It took a loose pass at the back from Dulwich Hamlet for us to take the lead - and you can guess which predator was alert to swoop in, Ashley Cheatley. She pops up having been quiet all half and guides the ball into the bottom corner. We were jubilant on the side, indicating that feeling of relief. To the contrary, the second half was substantially different. We were able to control extensive moments of the game and just like that Cheatley scored her second out of nothing. Capitalizing on a short pass from the back she spun her defender and with her left foot struck right into the top corner. An unstoppable strike to win the game, and the cup.

Things have not always been plain sailing - I remember losing our top goal scorer to Millwall Lionesses, of the Women's Super League in January 2017. To contextualize this, they were in the second tier of English football. This for me was a very emotional transfer. I had made her aware of Lionesses' approach in December, just before the Christmas break. She was interested, as I would expect any player to be, we were in Greater London Women's Football League division two, albeit in a comfortable position in the league and cups. There was an opportunity to leap from step eight to tier two - her dream of becoming a professional footballer was starring her in the face. Unbeknown to me, negotiations and contract discussions were going on behind the scenes. I told her my view that I didn't think this was a transfer she should make purely because of the vulnerable position Millwall were in financially, it's not something any player wants to be caught in the middle of. As well as this the travel wasn't so kind. She was a player that needed stability at a club, patience and trust. I didn't feel this was something she could be offered. Yes, from a selfish perspective I wanted to keep her, which manager wouldn't? But frankly I wanted the best and only the best for her. Either way my pleas fell on deaf ears and our cold-blooded sniper who had recorded fifty-one goals prior to her departure moved on. Now with her name on the back of her shirt and now wearing the number nine jersey, she was in new surroundings. A debut goal was always expected, and she did just that, social media went crazy, everyone sending their congratulations, I just couldn't bring myself to. I guess I was a little angry because from our conversations she was staying, it was twitter that notified me that she had officially signed. Hyperbole I had hoped but not quite, she was gone. As a club we had a ready-made goal-scorer in Sequoia Belworthy ready to take on the mantle, and she did not disappoint.

Cheatley went on to score the week after, but then an injury scampered things thereafter. Sidelined for a month and frustration at being benched weeks after just didn't sit right with her. At the end of the season she approached me about returning to Ashford, as transitioning her to a hold-up forward was not something she wanted. Of course there was so much more that played a part in her decision making, but ultimately she wanted to return home. It was as if the planets were aligned in terms of timing. Sequoia hung up her boots at the same time Cheatley wanted back in.

She fell out of love with football for a brief spell and if you saw her first training practice when she returned, you could tell it was just that. Her touch was off, she couldn't dribble - which was arguably her most protruding asset - she struggled to pass and more worryingly, simply had no recollection of how to hit the target. Matthew and I were startled; it took weeks for her to begin to look a shadow of her old self. But eventually, with patience and plenty of encouragement she was back to her best and ready for action. Development is a marathon, not a sprint. It is important to forecast the future whilst working on the technical, tactical, physical and psychological parts of an individuals game. We got there - her stats thereafter speaks volumes. An undeniably talented footballer who has grown with this football club and is only hitting her peak. Her future along with the football club are looking very bright indeed.

The Ferocious Machine, Ashley Cheatley.
Neil Cole

Signing for Millwall Lionesses.
Millwall Lionesses Media Team.

Back to her best in the infamous tangerine and white stripes, loving her football again. What a bundle of energy.

Chris Benn / Flickr

A special award for a special player. The first player to reach
the milestone of 100 games. In that time she scored 211 goals.
ATMFC

Ashley Cheatley with her mother Lisa Cheatley celebrating our
London & South East Regionals league victory in 2022.
Vikki Ovenell

CHAPTER

5

OUR FATE

"Even if Manchester United started a women's team to-morrow, they will have to begin at the very bottom and will have to work their way to the top, that's the association's rules and they will be bent for no one."

So you can imagine the dismay when the club's appointed secretary, Matt Corry, and I, stood before the Greater London Women's Football League Committee and our aspirations of being slipped into tier four were completely decimated. The hope stemmed from The London and South East Regional League secretary documenting; 'Having checked all the regulations and Pyramid Agreement, it is impossible for you to enter higher than Step 5, given that the squad you have listed is clearly a strong one

I hope that we can ensure that you enter the pyramid as close to the top of Step 5 as possible.' Taking this to the next training practice was simply to keep all participants informed but also subconsciously, to keep that fire burning and the dream alive. The hope was that these talented players at the peak of their careers would not have to wait at least half a decade to play National League football.

Back downstairs to the oubliette in the depths of a pub which presented more questions about the location than anything, was hardly a 'new club welcome', it was more of a dictatorship lounge which allowed the committee members to proudly dismiss our arguments. The unanimous feeling amongst the management at the club was simple. The squad was fiercely strong to begin at the bottom, too powerful for the teams we would potentially be competing against. It would not be fair to be on the receiving end of double-figure score lines, nor would our players gain any satisfaction from that. It's the study better known by researchers as 'The Goldilocks Effect', in which humans need to be effectively challenged in order for learning to take place. If the task is too easy, we get bored; if the task is too challenging we shut down in which little to no learning actually happens. We are constructed as human beings to avoid wasting cognitive resources on things too simple and too far out of our reach. This is our natural human instinct and the feeling was that this would apply when viewing just how strong of a squad the future Ashford Town (Middlesex) FC Women's team consisted of.

Collectively in that legroom, you would think as a community we would all share a common objective; to grow the women's game and successfully allow for participation to advance. Sorry to break it to you, but you are sorely mistaken. In fact what greeted us was a unified ambience of arrogance and stubbornness.

'So tell us what are you expecting from today?' the league's vice chair embraced us with.

Matt Corry and I exchanged a glance of confusion as the forwardness of the question hinted that a decision may already have been cast.

'Well having seen the strength of our squad, we were hoping to be in the Premier Division of the Greater London League' I hesitantly responded,

'What makes you think that could happen?' the aggressor returned with.

It is at this point a list of the players and the previous clubs they had represented were placed on desk, enough for each three committee members to individually assess. They didn't even courteously give us that respect. Instead, the man of the hour, uttered these words that rang so loud in my head that evening and again in the summer of 2018, only five days after my thirtieth.

"Even if Manchester United started a women's team tomorrow, they will have to begin at the very bottom and will have to work their way to the top, that's the association's rules and they will be bent for no one. You will begin in division three and there will be an opportunity for you to apply for accelerated promotion when the season is concluded." He robotically delivered this judgement without giving himself the opportunity to even breath. Maybe he was against the clock and was eager to see everyone, maybe happy hour was ending but the cynic in me was of the opinion that he simply couldn't wait to diminish our hopes.

We marched out of the room walking upstairs in single file to the exit as the next victims walked in the opposite direction ready for their ruling. The dreaded news we so desperately did not want chimed so loudly on the train journey home. How do I deliver this news to the players? Who on earth would stay at the club now? How long is this going to take before we get to compete effectively week after week, in the Women's National League?

The journey home felt like forever but it allowed me to plot a positive spin on the outcome provided. Our modern-day approach to playing the game, reinforced in our philosophy, was one we happily sketched as the ultimate attacking guide to football whilst displaying a strong understanding of how to defend effectively. It is one thing drawing this up, but it is another thing all together diligently animating this. I believed we possessed the quality of player to accomplish a lucrative style of playing, and superior coaches who possess the know-how to deliver this. It was not only the answer to promotion but a design to tactically outwit our opponents season after season. So I composed the Ashford Town (Middlesex) FC Women handbook, sat on the train. 50-pages of guidance about what we stand for, principles for coaching, example practices, and individual development plans. It was a case of preparing as best as possible, setting in place incredibly high standards in which those at the top had to operate at. It wasn't just the players I cared about developing, it was also those who shared the dugout with me.

Very soon after the verdict was cast, we welcomed everyone back to the training field, the environment was a jovial one and I had no ambition of destroying that pre or mid session. So as the players perched in a circle cooling down and stretching just before it was time to head home I delivered the dreaded news to the players.

"We have heard back from the league and unfortunately it's not the news we were expecting", the rest of the discourse continued in that vein, as I observed their clogs furiously reeling. Fortunately, I was not finished.

"Let's use this season as a means of proving to the league just what a mistake they have made, let's identify a way of playing and use the games to express ourselves in every way possible, let's use this as an opportunity to grow and not an excuse to collapse." Bear nodded powerfully, agreeably appealing to anyone with the slightest ounce of doubt.

This passionate sermon held sentiment for many but not for all. Eight participants withdrew their interest. Several returned to their former clubs whilst a portion pursued opportunities in the superior divisions. I forever respect the choice they made and still do to this day. As a football club we were left vulnerable and I have no doubt that this was a ploy to halt this journey but roadblocks were only seen as opportunities. This toughness was fixed into each member of this football club, with six members from the evolution continuing to represent the first team right the way through the divisions, but we needed reinforcements.

CHAPTER

6

VICTORY WITHOUT SUCCESS

Our first season in the Greater London Women's Football League was in the Southern region of division three. All in all, we did reasonably well in achieving our short term goal which was promotion, as league winners. We were able to solidify a style of play but never really felt we could experiment new ideas and strategies.

Maybe this was my fault? Once we begun competitive action, the pressure to fashionably fly through the divisions was inconspicuously fierce. This was pressure that I solely put onto myself, I must add. But why? Well I acutely concluded that in order to retain the quality in the squad then we needed to be winning. Winning is something players needed to feel to generate that sense of achievement, to substantiate progression and ultimately justify that Ashford was the place to be. This is what I told myself, so low and behold my coaching style referenced that. It was fiery, commanding, verging on being combustible. I cringe just at the thought.

We started off the season steam-rolling our competition and notching double figures. I shamefully demanded this. Brilliant for us but demoralizing for the opposition I'm sure. At one stage before a league game the opposition manager of Putney Vale Ladies, alluded to the fact we were far superior to the other teams in the division. Many were social teams who turn up to have a laugh with their friends whilst the others were new teams attracting players who were practically playing the game competitively for the very first time. The manager said himself he had spoken to the league about just how unjust and dejecting it was playing us. The women's game were, and continues to principally grow the number of participants. This was not the way to go about it. Every team we played in that division no longer operates today; Putney Vale, Hammersmith Starz, Club Langley, London Phoenix, Colne Valley, Orpington Ladies, Surrey Eagles, Carshalton Athletic, the list goes on and this speaks volumes. Of course the score lines seven years ago does not directly correlate to their eradication today however, it goes someway to justifying why we were deserving of beginning slightly higher than the very foot of the football pyramid. I learned a lot about winning in this league, the stimulation is like no other and I was addicted to this feeling. When we tasted defeat in the county cup final against University College London (UCL) FC, that was something else. Believe it or not I was reduced to tears. I was devastated. So used to winning, I shamefully forgot how to lose. We had opportunities to win the game but met an impressive goalkeeper who was invincible on the day. Although the ferocious machine was awarded player of the match with her well taken goals, this goalkeeper was another breed. Fearless in between the sticks and possessed handling teams at the very top level would be proud of.

I recognized tasting defeat was a weakness of mine, I hated losing so much it emotionally broke me. I stood and watched UCL lift the trophy and vowed never to taste this bitter pill again. I was determined that the next season things would be different so I sat down with the coaching team and begun concocting a plan for bigger and better for the succeeding season. We left no stone unturned; training needed to be improved, a divergent quality of player were required and we were coming for the lot, league, cups, you name it.

My expectations changed this new season, and frankly invested more into my coaching than ever before. Not financially, but intellectually. A manager lives in a world constantly full of deliberation, where results follow you throughout the entirety of your working week so I went back to the drawing board to read, watch, learn and observe to better my pedagogy.

It is hard to stand by your principles when things are not going as you want. This is why it is imperative to have a team who strive for excellence. I had Matthew Aumeeruddy, and have since built the senior management team to include Callum O'Connell, Tia Prior, Adam Frailing – all remarkable people. Both the manager and his cortège must work as one, and I have been lucky enough to work with this group who I trusted totally. If things were not quite tactically working in which teams found it easy to break us, then these coaches would be the first to advise on how we can be better. If my approach was too stern, our mental performance coach would instantly talk to me but from time to time I'd also get;

'I thought your talk after the match was so needed but also came across very powerful in my opinion. I felt you were able to put across how you felt effectively to the players and hopefully they will take that all in.'

These coaches were not just there to flatter me with words and say 'Yes Will!' they advised, helped and educated me. I always knew that the buck stopped with me, it's the manager who ultimately decides; he takes advice from everyone else but it is his final decision that counts and it is he who is praised or scorned for it. On game-day it is natural I will make some people unhappy, with my team selection, the more frequent this happens the more frustrating the player would feel and naturally begin to complain to everyone in the team, but you, the manager. Sometimes the players who are benched consistently would often complain about their teammates in their position. That's the energy that destroys teams and the toxic emotion that you don't want in the camp. I play the game myself, so I completely understand the fervency involved on a weekly basis. Considering these players pay membership fees to participate, it makes it even more challenging from a managerial perspective. Financially, they deserve to receive the identical playing experience as their fees are consistent. But only eleven can take to the field and unfortunately for many who have joined, broken away and relocated, it just wasn't for them. Some sauntered silently whilst some squawked sonorously. A wise man once told me that a bad apple creates an orchard and boy were these scattered seeds close to sprouting.

The succeeding football season threw a number of challenges our way. Our ruthless sniper left to join The Lionesses, we bounced from one training venue to another in the winter season because our funds simply didn't stretch to two hour practices at any of the local sites. I'm sure these are tests that other grassroots clubs had to and continue to struggle with. Most venues from the end of August, when we lose natural lighting book up faster than Christmas Party venues. We had to shift our training days on a number of occasions, just to be able to take the slots no one wanted. These were often a Monday, Wednesday and Friday, changing entirely our training schedule. The days available to us actively dictated what we could and could not do. For example, one month we opted for Monday and Wednesday training, as it was an assumption that no one would ever arrive to a Friday practice. Never assume as it could make an... you know the rest. Anyway, because we would play our matches on a Sunday afternoon, Monday training could only be a recovery session. One part would be reflecting on the game from the day before, but mostly it would be led by our strength and conditioning coach, in which players would focus on a range of stretches combined with some running, ensuring the load was overly heavy. Players needed to understand the importance of their bodies recovering well from the hardship of matchday, to prevent injuries and aid in reducing fatigue, so we took this seriously. This was vital in reducing the risk of short-term injuries like ankle tweaks to the more interminable ones such as an ACL. This then meant Wednesday's practice would allow us to deliver pattern practices, phases of play - practices that looked like the game we experienced on a Sunday that meant we could tactically ameliorate our game. We often shoved in there advanced technical practices to ensure we didn't neglect individual advancement.

It sounds like we had every planned, right down to the last notch, but I will be lying to you. Most weeks we battled with location and worse yet unavailability. My biggest bugbear, which remains, are the last minute drop-outs. A sign of a good teacher is their ability to adapt to whatever is thrown at them, we found ourselves adapting all of the time. One practice we had four players turn up. You can bet we ran the practice, and made the best of time we had with the players. I would often read the players the riot act after a game on Sunday, not so much now. I've learnt it is far more effective for players to hold their teammates accountable for not attending, these changes were reflective in our results.

Despite training causing so much pain, we were able to muddle through the football season, winning the league, county cup and the league cup. The treble was made sweeter when we won the league cup defeating Hammersmith Starz 3-2 at the Beveree, the home of Hampton and Richmond Borough Football Club. We were 2-0 down at half time and I remember the team talk at the interview as clear as day. The players sat down nervously, I can't tell you why because I was never an aggressor in the changing rooms. It was our safe space. I was never one to give the players the hair-dryer treatment, never one to send boots flying across the room - maybe this simply was a sign that we were all immune to losing, anxiety was naturally the next best emotion. I serenely sat down amongst the players in the away changing facilitates, composed myself and sedately spoke.

'I would like you all to please just take a deep breath'...we unanimously begun to inhale and exhale, you couldn't hear it, you could just feel it.

'I would like you all to relax out there in the second half. Calm down and start to play football like we have done all season. Go and express yourselves; wide forwards take on your full backs and put them under untold amounts of stress, Charmaine, drive at the defenders, very few can live with you when you do that. Please remember if we lose today it is just a football match, the world keeps on spinning, but please do not come back in at the end of the game and feel you could have done more.' That was it.

We returned having turned the game on it's head, clawed back a two-goal deficit and left victorious.

It has gone on to serve us very well in building this football club. Winning division three was brilliant but it was division two that was the test as well as success. We were convincingly unbeaten in the league but it was the Christmas break when we were really tested; we lost the ferocious machine to Millwall Lionesses in the Women's Super League. That's right, despite our superior league position, and promotion all but guaranteed, our top goal scorer got her move to the big time while as a coaching team we were totally unprepared to lose a player of that calibre, at this stage of the season anyway. This transfer was one I did not like at all. Maybe I was a little bitter but I recall receiving a phone call from the manager at the time who was desperate to sign her. I have no doubt conversations went on without my knowledge because the last I heard she was staying put. Only for a press release a few days later confirming they have sealed the signature of our top goal scorer.

Many amateur managers who lose a player go on a tirade, I did the opposite and said nothing. Despite feeling rancorous over it, I channeled this emotion into improving the squad we had. She scored on her debut in the WSL and twitter went pretty crazy over it all. I just couldn't muster up the courage to congratulate her, I felt so deceived. Last week she was staying, a week later she was grabbing the winner in the Women's FA Cup for The Lionesses. Eventually, a day later, I congratulated her and that was the last time we spoke that season. Winning the first two league games of the season, after Cheatley moved on, helped eradicate any fears of a dip in the road and we somewhat managed to unearth a hidden gem in the process in Sequoia Belworthy.

For me this season was winning at its best, to lose such a potent threat in the opposition box is difficult; irrelevant of the level of football you compete at, it is always an unimaginable challenge to replace goals. Yet, we never felt defeated. Disappointed yes, but never defeated. I sauntered into training on Tuesday night, hands in my pocket as I disrupted the crinkled sheet of paper with names and positions jotted down, ready for the practice. I paced up and down the same strip of turf guardedly wearing away what was left of it wondering how the players would react, curious of their reactions and planning the inspirational sermon I would deliver this time to ensure nothing derailed our progress.

'Of course by now you've all heard and seen the news' I said sternly.

'But I want nothing to stop this run we're on this season. We're top of the league for a reason, still unbeaten, in every cup and can make this our most successful season yet'.

The players knew I was right, and I felt they digested every ounce of what I was saying. This just shows the personalities I had the pleasure of working with because this must have been tough for them. With this mental toughness combined with their individual quality I knew just how memorable they could make the season. This was to be an extraordinary year.

I tried not to overdo it in the first game back, I didn't feel the added pressure was necessary. It was key to keep the preparation simple and the pre-match team talk calm and stress-free.

A few were in tentative spirits and you could see it in how we started the game, but the beauty of the sport is that once you get a touch of the ball, all the anxieties disappear. Sequoia grabbed her hatrick but it was Lavana Neufville who impressed. A player who has been with the club since it formed and remains one of my favourite players at the football club. Honest, quality and always seems to raise her game year after year. Lavana would go on to represent Middlesex County and be runner-up to *the machine* as the clubs all-time leading goal scorer. Technically, she has never been the best on the ball but tactically is highly intelligent. Physically, how she managed to perform as well as she has over the years will forever be a mystery to me because I am positive she has missed every conditioning practice we've held. I guess miracles really do happen! She had a tough start to life and I think all the time just how lucky I am to have played a small part in how things have transitioned for her.

Lavana Neufville, one of the clubs greatest ever goal-scorers.
Neil Cole

Delivering information to players during an interval in a GLWFL
Division 3 (South) fixture.

Gary Paul

THAT DISASTROUS SEASON

Greater London Women's Football League division two champions, league cup winners and county cup victors. But the good times wouldn't last.

As the old saying goes, if you fail to plan, you are planning to fail.

This new league season just didn't feel the same. On one hand it was always going to be a challenge to replicate a treble winning season but on the other I had the feeling that we simply did not prepare for this season as typically we would do. Quintessentially, we would sit down as a coaching and management team, discuss the individuals in the team and highlight areas we needed to cover or urgently needed to strengthen. This didn't happen. In management terms this is called complacency. My ever-attentive assistant who is heedful of situations that may appear in the season warned the squad was light on the ground and an injury away from scratching our heads on the touchline about where to go next. He wasn't wrong. In one respect I should be grateful for this horrific season which saw us finish third in the league below our intimate rivals; New London Lionesses and Godalming Town.

Some called it a love triangle, I simply couldn't stand the two rivals who always gave us a torrid time against them. From a personal perspective, the coaches were great but from a competitive standpoint they were very much formidable rivals. They always roughed us up and we always seemed to accept it.

The 2016/17 season was always going to be a step up in terms of the competitiveness we were faced with each week, we felt it. There always appeared to be a softness to us. As a coaching team, we worked hard to eradicate this, but being street wise enough is something you either have or don't have. Godalming didn't just possess quality players in their side, there was an intelligence to their game; where to give away free kicks, where to win free kicks; how to get the officials where they wanted them and on that odd occasion how to frustrate our players. One season we had to travel to Godalming away from home - we had a reasonably strong squad but being a grassroots team that tend to play matches on a Sunday, not everyone could commit to playing this midweek fixture. So we travelled a few players light, but still of the belief we had enough to win the game. The referee denied us a stonewall penalty in the opening few minutes of the game when Neufville was clawed down in the box. Moments later Cheatley was then hacked down, again nothing given and this appeared to wrangle our counterparts in the dugout, so much so one bellowed out;

'She's always diving, it's no wonder Millwall didn't want you!' - my jaw hit the floor, at the same time I wanted to march over there. I knew better of it. This one time anyway.

What a low blow. From this moment no matter the capacity we met in, I viewed them all differently. It was a shame because they consisted of some talented football-ers, one I went on to sign in Jade Johnson - a key member of our promotion winning side in 2022. We drew this game in the end but that's a moment I won't ever forget. To be honest, I don't believe Cheatley even heard him clamor this, until now of course.

New London Lionesses were not like this, they con-sisted of a highly qualified and intelligent coach in Glenn Shimmins, a good team, but a fully fit Ashford side were a better team. They played in a way that would pose any team difficulties and I'm sure one season they took Ipswich Town all the way to a penalty shoot-out in the Women's FA Cup. Their strategy whenever we played them was to sit deep, soak up pressure and hit us on the counter attack.

Godalming were different in their approach. They often brought the game to us. They had a good setup, definitely appeared to be a team that were geared for the higher level. Steve Davies was a great guy, he relished the rivalry and enjoyed our clashes. The less said about the other coaches, the better but what we all had was a competitive streak, frankly it's what added fuel to the fire. Upon reflection, this is arguably where it went wrong for me. There is no doubting that the main duty of a coach is to best prepare their players and give them the best possible chance of success; this particularly season the team were to pay the price for underestimating our familiar foes.

As a team we were disappointed and desperate to find out how exactly we transitioned to this. The players, the coaches and to a large extent our spectators all wanted answers as well as solutions. That is exactly what I strived to give them. A team that would win the GLWFL Premier Division as well as the London and South East Regional Premier Division. No one was going to stand in my way and I refused to take no for an answer; from anyone.

The winner and runner-up in the division achieved promotion naturally to the top division and as third place finishers we were required to complete an application form for accelerated promotion. Now we really were at the mercy of the GLWFL committee and I wasn't going to let my pride get in the way of things this time.

1. Finishing Position of the Team

We are proud our players continue to surpass expectations every season after successive promotions and multiple cup success against teams of higher standing.

2. Playing Record of the Team

Our modest squad continue their commitment to have fun together on and of the pitch frequently outperform teams in superior leagues. Our squad successfully competed in the FA Cup (reaching the first round proper) whilst challenging for the league with the least players of any Division One team. Multiple players consistently represent Middlesex County FA.

3. Administration Record

Administration is and continues to be of a high standard. Only an incident this season where County FA were awaiting a players address which saw us expelled from a Cup (player represented County team). We abide by league and FA rules with an unblemished record otherwise. The following week the FA issued an apology to all Clubs for messages not being sent to Clubs but disqualified our team without the opportunity to discuss and subsequently we are without funds to appeal. Our reputation and integrity is critical to our responsibility, hence my personal upset at the refusal of the FA for any interaction until outcome decided.

4. Facilities

Following all the Club's success since its beginning, recent additions across the club include extending our comprehensive training schedule (training twice a week) and creating a junior section for three age groups (U12s, U14s & U16s). This development pathway is laid for the foundation for the future with plans for a Reserve Team to build on the momentum and local community interest to 'grow the game' and the FA objective to double participation in 2020. Our Club's sustained success is steered by our specialist coaches and complimented and powered by the continued support of the pitch. This includes: individual tailored fitness programmes delivered by a dedicated Sports & Conditioning Coach and, since our inaugural season, the benefit of a Physiotherapist to protect against injuries and aid recovery from a demanding schedule. From the outset the long term vision secured a category-C venue with:

- floodlights to first team pitch and training pitch
- club House and bar
- seated accommodation for 250 supporters
- covered standing accommodation for a further 250 supporters
- post and rail surround to first team pitch
- concrete walkway around all four sides of the pitch
- a large dressing room and referee changing facilities
- first aid accommodation and dedicated medical room with treatment table.

On behalf of the players, coaches and our supporters, we are sincerely grateful for your time to consider our application and welcome further questions at any time.

In trust,
Ashford Town (Middx) LFC

Yes our tails were between our legs at this stage, but the hope was that the league would see the journey we had been on, the facilities we fortunately possessed at the club, and just how bright our future looked. The hope was that they would see this season as a one-off, results wise anyway. Weeks and months went by and still our fate had yet to be decided. This was no surprise; they moved at snail pace for you but at rapid speed against you! One year a fine was emailed through because the corner flags were not placed in before the referee arrived - make of that as you will.

The league eventually emailed through the constitution for the new season and there we were - under the GLWFL Premier Division's list of teams, along with our two familiar, cutthroat rivals. I was delighted to see us propel, albeit through our accelerated promotion application, it was good to progress and important from a club perspective that we didn't stand still.

Teaching and learning never stops.
ATMWFC

Tactically reaffirming what we required from our strike-force as we locked horns against Godalming in the cup, the only time we defeated them this season.
ATMWFC

CHAPTER

8

SPRING SERIES

An unprecedented, but predicted, global pandemic had ravaged the country. In fact, COVID-19 spread across the world, forcing governments to execute their very own safe-guarding measures to subsequently save lives, protect their economies and shield their health systems from the im-pact of the epidemic. As a result, the impact on 'non-elite' football in England denoted the suspension of fixtures and training across all levels of the game. The decision was made as the government announced a lockdown, meaning grassroots football was no longer permitted.

The excitement of promotion to the London and South East Regionals was short lived because at the halfway point, the season was curtailed and declared null and void.

Of course, the health and safety of the general public was paramount and football was secondary to lives. Yet somehow, the season felt like it ended all too prematurely. Sitting in fourth place with twenty points, it was a compelling opening campaign.

Fast-forward one year, we were still in a nationwide lockdown. News however, had emerged that re-starting grassroots football were being discussed at state level in line with the easing of lockdown restrictions on gatherings, public spaces and other outdoor activities. The excitement was simply unparalleled. We had spent so much time decoding our games from the season just nullified, meeting with individuals on zoom to analyze their game performance with a fine toothpick, as well coming up with a range of methods to improve ourselves as a coaching team. We were now just ready to get back out on the grass. The return of grassroots football is something that we know many were undeniably joyous about, but at this stage of the nation's response to COVID-19, so much careful consideration was put into this "phased return", for everyone's safety, especially vulnerable groups. This was however the moment the country had hoped for, a return to normality. With this, came regulations we had to get right as a club. We needed to ensure we only returned when we had the appropriate measures in place as developed by The FA. This meant:

- We needed to identify a Covid-19 officer who will be responsible for developing a Covid-19 plan.
- We needed to compose a general safeguarding risk assessment before re-starting, and have this displayed on our website.
- We needed to establish a Covid-19 group to be responsible for producing and implementing this risk assessment, and overseeing the safe return.

This was not an easy project but something we were patently strict on. We missed the game and understand the seriousness that beleaguered the guidance so we did nothing to put anyone at risk. The guidance was sketched and we were ready to go, yet again.

Individual training started, and players were filling up our calendars like you wouldn't believe. I know they missed football but boy was there a spirited drive to get back to what they loved the most. I felt it. So we did, we were back out training in small groups mindful of those who were apprehensive in returning to the game. The news followed shortly after that football was to return and the league campaign would begin for the new football season. Our opening game was a trip away to Dartford. Missing our ferocious finisher and an early injury to our dominant defender Anya Kinnane, felt as though lady luck was not on our side. Low and behold we lost 2-0, it was a bitter journey back home that evening.

We were never down for too long, the spirit that we bred into this team was unparalleled. And that was proven winning the remaining league and cup games. But that success was short-lived because following concerns that the four-tier system was not containing the spread of the virus, national restrictions were reintroduced for a third time in January.

The rules during the third lockdown meant people were once again told to stay at home. With the continued disruption caused by the COVID-19 pandemic, it was the premature end to another terse campaign. The FA decided to curtail the 2020-21 season with immediate effect so this time, the FA used this opportunity to restructure the football pyramid, increasing the number of teams in the superior divisions. Consequently, the Women's Football Board used this as an opportunity to allow clubs to apply to move up into the tier immediately above their current tier within the Women's Football Pyramid. We applied, and believed that applications were marked on the following criteria:

On-Field (75%)

- Points per games across 2019/20 and 2020/21 (55%)
- FA Cup performance in 2019/20 and 2020/21 (10%)
- League Cup performance in 2019/20 (5%)
- League Goal Difference in 2019/20 and 2020/21 (5%)

Off-Field (25%)

- Club Structure (5%)
- Workforce (5%)
- Facilities (5%)
- Finance (5%)
- Administration (5%)

Whilst we patiently awaited our fate, our league announced a 'non-competitive' L&SERWFL Spring Round Robin series. Players were enlivened just to compete again, no matter the format. Following on from the government's plans in March, to begin a phased exit from lockdown, there was finally light at the end of a long-drawn-out tunnel. We were back playing. We were so ambitious, we saw this competition as our opportunity to write a few wrongs. We were combative, many would say. We kicked-off with an away victory to Saltdean, followed by successful results against Eastbourne Town, Dartford, Dulwich Hamlet and QPR, it was a win ratio that left us delighted, it propagated *hope,* hope that our accelerated promotion application might yet be a successful one. 'Having defeated every team that had also applied, surely it's ours?' I'd often say to boss-man Matthew.

- Saltdean United 1 - 1 Ashford FC Women
- Eastbourne Town 3 - 5 Ashford FC Women

- Dartford Women 1 - 3 Ashford FC Women
- Dulwich Hamlet 2 - 3 Ashford FC Women
- QPR Women 1 - 8 Ashford FC Women

'Just look at these results, surely! We've defeated every team who have applied to go up.'

Low and behold, the email flashed on my Apple Watch which gave off a vibration, my phone momentarily followed, before my iPad obliged to the notification. The opening 'Upward Club Movement Application - Under Embargo Until 16.00 on Wednesday' is all the alert would reveal. My sweaty palms had to wait that extra bit longer as my passcode began to evade me. At the third time of dabbing, I was in. I couldn't compose myself to read it word for word and jumped straight to the outcome...

'Your team's application for Upward Club Movement has been assessed by the FA Women's Football Board and I can confirm that your application was not successful on this occasion.'

That was all I read. I forwarded the email straight to Matthew and got that sinking feeling at the pit of my stomach, the same after I received the Manchester United tirade. I begun to wonder just how to tell these spirited players who held just as much hope as I did. The message went straight into the players' WhatsApp group and the messages started flooded in, shock, frustration, disappointment and anger.

Everything I expected from a group driven to compete at the highest possible level, this fueled our next chapter.

We spent days on our application to ensure it was ideal for presentation and quintessentially ready, only for a solitary line to forge our feedback: 'On-Field Criteria (PPG, FA Cup performance, League Cup performance, Goal Difference)'. That was it, but it sure was enough to shape our reflection on the COVID-stricken seasons, and without further restrictions in place would finally allow us to complete a first full season it the London and South East Regionals. We were powered and read to go and assemble history.

What winning the spring series meant to the team. This was
after our away victory to Dulwich Hamlet.

Liam Asman

THE INVINCIBLES

I always expected promotion to go to the very end

Like us, Fulham, Saltdean and Dulwich Hamlet all improved their squads in summer and the latter would have felt a sense of frustration at being overlooked for promotion to The Women's National League. But I was prepared better than ever this season. Whilst defeating every team in the spring series competition instilled confidence, it was the breakthrough players that series who really gave me the belief that this was going to be a special season. We were going to shock people - we were going to achieve something quite remarkable.

A few departed before the season officially begun which no doubt created a sense of uncertainty. Every coach knows it's a nightmare when players simply are not straight with you. They want transparency and honesty from you but fail to live by these standards. Seven years in, it still leaves me perplexed. This mini clear out mind you took me back to a few years ago when the 'bad apples' departed. Not that these were any trouble at all but it left spaces for players with new ideas, changed mindsets and alternative qualities. Something every forward-think coach looking to progress their squad looks for. I was no different.

A seven-day approach came in for a player, who since her arrival, was not getting as much game time as she would have maybe expected. She was a player who had experience in The National League and one that wanted to progress with a club on the rise. Our demands were parallel, so it made sense to work together but I just never felt either gave one another a chance. I didn't ever give Hannah the run of games a player would require to generate a relationship with their teammates, or the opportunity to fail without judgement. Instead, she had me pugnaciously barking from the dugout. Nevertheless her fortunes of course changed and in no time she found herself on her feet in the WNL with Stevenage Women FC who she went on to captain. A number of players fell into this category over the years, of having left leaving me with a contrast of emotions. Frustrated at the little they had to offer, yet hopeful of their future in the game.

Months went by and the new football season dawned on us. A few more players were in the squad for a game or two then never returned for sometime, as well as ones who infrequently attended training practices, before never returning. I would receive that dreaded Whatsapp message...

'Hi Will, first off I wanted to start by saying... Here we go I'd mumble before scouring through the rest. 'I have been offered an opportunity to play higher...I would like to wish you the best for the season'.

If phones could compress, I would have got through my fair few by now. Not to evade the ex girlfriends either, just out of sheer frustration of players misleading me. Whilst this was frustrating, it allowed me to wear my professional hat, it allowed us as a coaching and management team to know exactly what we needed for the new season. Our core players remained; right through the crux of the team were Sophie Shults, Anya Kinnane, Kalani Peart, Alissa Down, Lavana Neufville and Ashley Cheatley. A brawny spine. Burly. Bullish. Bloody brilliant.

Surrounded were breakthrough players who bided their time and absorbed a lot; taking their opportunity when it presented itself. Energetic Ellen Clarabut and the dutiful Laura Huse who has been an ever-present participant since its inception, made up the defensive unit. The retuning Rozalia Sitarz, and Jade Johnson held the wing back spots, Jordanne Hoesli-Atkins and Chloe Farrell often transitioned in the middle of the pitch, before Ruby Linton returned to shake things up. This side very rarely changed and I firmly believe it's this consistency that led to the club achieving its most successful season in history.

How was our luck? We were drawn Dartford in the opening five league games of the season, and this time we knew the battle that was ahead of us. We seized on the momentum from the spring series and recognized the importance of winning all of our games leading up to the big showdown against the Darts. We obliterated the teams that stood in our way:

Ashford Town (Middx) 9-1 Millwall Lionesses
Ashford Town (Middx) 8-1 Aylesford
Saltdean United 2-5 **Ashford Town (Middx)**
Ashford Town (Middx) 4-2 New London Lionesses

We were winning in some style, but there was a feeling amongst the MDT that we were conceded far too many goals to effectively mount a grave title charge. So leading up to the clash many dubbed as the ultimate battle we focused our training on defending. Dartford's strategy was a direct style of football, which they were highly successful in so defending the long ball, was our focus on Friday's training practice. I drew sessions from my 'developing defenders' coaching course I sat at St George's Park, England's National football centre purposely built for coaching and development, information that formed the very foundation of the ever-evolving blueprint that continued to serve us so well.

We drilled into the team that defending was a team effort, as well as a team responsibility so we broke this down to the players in recognizing how and when to adopt out of possession:

1. A high press
2. A mid-block
3. Defending deep

All three look completely different and the responsibility of individuals' shift changed with each of these different demands. But with defending, players also needed to recognize in possession how and when to:

1. Manage momentum
2. Play forward
3. Attack quickly

This formed the basis of our practice design, in which the players perfectly applied. I spoke to the MDT at the culmination of the practice and repeated the same messages before kick-off on Sunday 19th September 2022.

'It is so important that we trust the players to execute exactly what's required and trust the process'.

The coaches simultaneously nodded in agreement, without a single objection. They believed in these group of players just as much as I did, they were convinced by the training practice that these group of players were ready and well equipped. They weren't wrong. Our steely-striker stole the show recording a fine hatrick of goals but it was our resilient defending that had satisfied me and our ability to manage crucial moment in the game with great intelligence. As we suffer We had defeated Dartford 3-2 with the score line arguably flattering our opponents as they notched a free-kick with the last kick of the game. It was a pleasing result but ultimately we cognized just how this positive score-line was to send a firm message out to the rest of our competition. We meant business this season.

The season perused in this vain as we continued to entertain with some exceptional football, in the process:

Ashford Town (Middx) 8-0 Worthing Women
Dulwich Hamlet 1-1 **Ashford Town (Middx)**
Ashford Town (Middx) 4-1 Denham United
Denham United 1-6 **Ashford Town (Middx)**
Ashford Town (Middx) 1-1 Fulham FC
Millwall Lionesses 0-4 **Ashford Town (Middx)**

Ashford Town (Middx) 2-0 Dartford FC
Ashford Town (Middx) 3-0 Saltdean United
New London Lionesses 1-6 **Ashford Town (Middx)**

On 27th March 2022 we hosted Dulwich Hamlet in the league. This was a tough game for two reasons; one being they held genuine quality all over the pitch and the other being they were one of two sides who we had not beaten in the league thus far. I was focused on this game but I had one eye on Fulham's game as they hosted Dartford. We needed nine points to win the league but with other results going our way promotion could be secured sooner than first predicted.

Typical of us this season we started at a frightening pace and created a number of goal-scoring opportunities. Dulwich had their fair few also and caused us problems in the final third but it was our dependable servant Lavana Neufville who popped up just before the half-time interval and slotted the ball in after impressive combination play in and around the eighteen-yard box. It was what we call in football, the perfect time to score and settle any nerves or doubts that may have subconsciously squirmed in. Half an hour before the final whistle, guess who popped up again? Our rapid, ruthless, record-breaker... Ashley Cheatley. She raced through the defensive line and tucked the ball into the bottom corner, Cheatley style. On the side-lines, we all stumbled to a huge sigh of relief, but this shortly turned to jubilation when other results were back in. Dartford had earned a hard-fought 1-0 victory away to our title nemesis Fulham. We only required four points to win the league in our remaining four games.

We now travelled away to Worthing FC Women knowing a victory would put us in touching distance of the trophy we all coveted. Tia Prior has been the clubs mental performance coach for the past two seasons, and been an addition I am delighted to have made. She has run workshops in-person and virtually, through video conference especially when COVID-19 dictated everyone's life. The workshops were nothing short of effective and inspirational, touching on topics like:

· What is Sport Psychology?
· Team cohesion
· Performance profiles
· Self confidence and positive thinking
· Goal setting

And it's the latter, that mental training technique that increased the drive and commitment in achieving what we did this season. We set three different types of goals; our first being out outcome goals - which we said was our main goal - winning the league, remaining undefeated and winning the league as well as the Combined Counties Cup.

Then it was time to set or performance goals, in brief these were what we needed to do to reach our ultimate objective and finally were our process goals. These were what training we needed to do to reach the performance standards. These are great and some may think these were discussed and nothing ever came of it but not Tia. These were visible above everyone's seat in the changing rooms, these were referred to in team talks and even more powerful, these were personal to the individual. These goals had three instrumental effects; they enhanced performance; increased confidence and ultimately they focused and often refocused.

Outcome Goals

- Win the league and be promoted.
- remain undefeated in the league.
- win the league and the midweek cup.

Performance Goals

- Score at least two goals in a game (as a team).
- At least seven clean sheets out of nine remaining league games.
- Every player should have clarity on their roles for set pieces.
- Attend 6/8 training sessions a month per player.

- Once every six weeks, organize a social.

Process Goals

- Defend as a team.
- Be more clinical in front of goal.
- Clear communication and preparation as a unit for set-pieces.
- Do not drop out of training on the day.
- If a session is missed, make up for it outside of training - provide evidence.

Many ask how consecutive promotions and sustained success have been achieved, frankly its the evolution of a high-performance environment where players hold each other accountable, and want nothing more than to hit the targets they set themselves, this was the secret behind it all. So when we travelled away to Worthing, a Worthing side that only a month ago disconcertedly knocked us out of the League Cup. The less said about how they thwarted us, the better. We knew only a victory would do. Despite a nervy start, we won the game 5-0. We were not joyous as a result of the performance, it was having gained three points because now were a meagre victory away from promotion and being crowned league champions. It was Whyteleafe Women who stood in our way of premature celebrations but we knew the job at hand when we travelled to the borough of Croydon. It appeared to some a straight forward job but I can assure you it was not. Whyteleafe were fighting for survival, fighting to maintain their status in the London and South East Regionals. But I echoed one message to the players, 'it's now or never'.

The pressure was not due to my desperation to be a national league side, at least not this time. The regionals premier was rapidly becoming increasingly competitive with every year that elapsed.

But these group of athletes were prepared - for the very first time ever, I felt this group did not need me one bit. They did not need my words of wisdom, nor did they need me to tactically educate them; our inculcate approach over the past months had been invaluable. Players arrived for the scheduled team meet, came out for their warm up in a timely manner, full of energy like you wouldn't believe. I cannot remember our preparation being this flawless but these players were ready. The momentum provided us with a competitive advantage but it was that drive from the players that allowed this day to piece things all together. Six months ago was the last time we had notched double figures against our opposition, that was a 25-0 victory over Highworth Town, in The Vitality Women's FA Cup, as social-media erupted.

'Wow!'

'What a result!'

'Why?'

'Did the other team even field a team or were you playing the under 10s so bang 25 goals?'

'Has to be a record'

'Sorry...did I see that right... 25 goals? Holy mother of fish cakes!'

'OMG'

'Close match then'

'Why print this, it's not fair on the other team.'

Some of the comments were interesting, with one in particular insinuating we should feel embarrassed over this score-line. I can assure you, these winners felt nothing of the sort. They were delighted, and so they should be. Months later double digits were up for all to see yet again. This time is was to officially be crowned champions of the London and South East Regionals division, winning

10-0 against Whyteleafe, with four games still to spare. Suddenly it all just felt real, our oppositions thereafter provided us with a guard of honor. We felt like champions. We were champions with an incomparable record. Winning the London and South East Regional League, County Cup and Combined Counties Cup. A treble winning season never to be forgotten.

P - 20   W- 18   D - 2   L - 0   GD - 81   PTS - 56

The squad had spent an excessive amount of time discussing, setting and inevitably delivering these standards, goals, ideas, objectives and blueprint. Year after year, building blocks were placed to prepare us and ultimately propel us to this level. It was an ever-changing blueprint composed seven years ago because it allowed us to add innovative ways of working towards success, and take away content we felt were stale, outdated and could impede our long term objectives.

I mention *we* an awful lot in here, at times it will link to the players and I as one big family. Other times, it's in reference to Matthew Aumeeruddy and I. The genius behind a lot. It can't be easy to be second in command, nor can it be that easy to work with someone like me, my better half may testify. Matthew does both. I truly hope *bossman*, I affectionally allude to my assistant as, continues to make strides in the professional game. He deserves to work at the highest tier possible, as a number one. My only wish when he does is that he finds a second in command as brilliant as him.

7 YEARS

84 MONTHS

2,556 DAYS

61,344 HOURS

3,680,640 MINUTES

220, 838, 400 SECONDS.

CHAPTER

10

THE NEXT CHAPTER

After winning 5-0 away to Worthing FC Women, we were one step closer to promotion, this was huge.

James Boyes / Flickr

Whyteleafe Women welcoming the champions elect onto the pitch, in the last game of the season with a guard of honour.
Vikki Ovenell

Lucy Potter and I lifting our long awaited league trophy. As a team, we partied long into the night, despite our county cup final 48 hours later.

Vikki Ovenell

Skipper, Alissa Down lifting the Capital Women's Cup, the
second trophy lift of the season.
Chris Benn

Winning the Combined Counties Midweek Cup.
Neil Cole

With my right hand man, Matthew Aumeeruddy. Lifting the Combined Counties Midweek Cup. What a journey we have both been on.

Neil Cole

**Kalani and Sophie reminding everyone just how many trophies
we lifted in our 2021/22 campaign. Never forget.**

Neil Cole

THE BLUEPRINT

Ashford Town (Middx) Girls & Women's F.C

Raising Standards

OUR PHILOSOPHY IS TO PLAY FOOTBALL WITH AN EFFICIENT & EFFECTIVE ATTACK MINDED APPROACH, WHERE PASS QUALITY, SUPPORT & MOVEMENT LEAD TO PENETRATION IN THE FINAL THIRD, TO CREATE GOAL-SCORING OPPORTUNITIES.

TABLE OF CONTENTS

OUR PHILOSOPHY ALLOWS AND ENCOURAGES YOU TO DISPLAY CREATIVITY AND CONTRIBUTE TO THE ATTACKING PHASE WITH VARIETY, COURAGE AND WITH CONSIDERED RISK TAKINGS

WELCOME

Welcome to your Resource Pack for the new football season. This pack is written to help you to understand the expectation as an individual at this football club. It will also act as a reference for you throughout the football season.

Our goal at Ashford Town (Middlesex) is to create a winning senior culture whilst allowing for players to develop and fulfil their potential in a patient, fun, enjoyable, positive yet highly challenging environment. Within this goal we are looking for all teams to work in correspondence with each other by playing football in an identical style however having dissimilar approaches to the game.

Our youth teams are at a development stage of their personal development, so it is important everyone embraces the approach all coaches and members of the management share. We are NOT and will not accept a "win at all costs" approach. It is important to recognize and understand that part of the learning process is to allow young students of the game to explore and take risks in all positions of the pitch without the pressure of doing things "the traditional way". Here at the football club I want to develop independent thinkers and excellent decision makers of the game with creativity as well as an unorthodox approach to playing football. In the youth phase especially, this is not something that can be done alone. Just like every player on the football pitch, each person associated with this football club has a role to play. This can be viewed in the inspiring our young players section. Winning football matches are ideal and sometimes it shows progression is taking place however winning or losing is not a way to solely measure player development. Win, lose, or draw, be positive and consistently encourage players (because it is about them) and watch individuals blossom.

Ashford Town (Middlesex) Women are success driven. Standing still means we get left behind the competition, so it is our aim and your challenge to build on this success. The coaching team are passionate in raising the standards of everyone that is involved with this football club ensuring that the football being played at the senior level is being mirrored at the junior level. For this to happen the senior sides must set high standards of themselves and set an example to all, especially the youth groups, as we look to create stronger cohesion amongst the teams. Our modern-day approach to coaching, reinforced in our philosophy, will reflect in the type of attacking football we demand whilst displaying a strong understanding of how to defend effectively.

I for one am very excited for this season ahead because I believe we have the quality of players in the squad to accomplish a lucrative style of play, possess superior coaches who have a passion to continuously learn and improve game by game and practice by practice and parents who share, embrace and understand the direction in which this football club as a whole is heading in. I hope that you find this pack useful and wish you all good luck for the season ahead.

Thank you,
Will Boye

PLAYER CHARACTERISTICS

Talented and gifted individuals are those that match the characteristics illustrated. It is our goal to develop, nurture and produce players to this standard. We believe these are the characteristics of a top performer which you have the capability to be if you are not already.

Creative: produces original ideas

"Playing football without care of outcome is preferable to caring too much"

Players are encouraged to bring plenty of creativity to every game and practice. Produce skills that you express in the playground or in the park. The football pitch is your stage.

Display imagination and inventiveness

An important attacking principle of play is 'innovation, use your football brain to come up with skills and trickery that evades the opposition. Practice things in training, such as bicycle kicks, overhead kicks, diving headers, you name it. These are my examples, come up with your own original ideas also.

Prepare to experiment and risk being wrong

Football is a beautiful sport that must be enjoyed first and foremost. To enjoy your football, you need to be confident in yourself to experiment. Utilize the learning method of trial and error. Not just in training but also on match day. Risk taking is what we encourage, predominantly in the youth phases because it acts as a learning tool as well as a successful way of demonstrating creativity.

Learning focused: like new challenges

Embrace challenges and approach them with a can-do attitude.

Master information quickly

Never look at practices or match days in isolation, as separate or standalone experiences. Process advice and information that is given quickly and re-call on your wide range of knowledge and know how to make excellent decisions. Every training practice is a teaching practice so soak in every bit of information players and coaches provide.

Students of the game

Be self-motivated students of the game. Have an underlying passion for the sport and for the football club. There is no substitute for passion, hard work and determination. Attend football matches, at different levels, to assess a variety of ways the game can be played. Watch players who play in similar positions to you to learn ways you can improve your game. Never stop learning.

Motivated and passionate: strive for high standards

Top players never rest on their laurels. They always want to progress and build on performances in practice and match days. Ooze class and professionalism ensure that the club is always being represented with the highest degree of respect.

Set SMART goals and targets

Set personal goals and targets to ensure that they are achievable and challenge you to become a better player. Football is a team game so try to set challenges with the team in mind. For example, setting a challenge to score 30 goals in the season is brilliant, however, this target shouldn't affect the support you offer your team-mates and your role and responsibility on the pitch. Goals that you set must be Specific, Measurable, Attainable, Relevant and Time-based.

Evaluative

Self-critiquing and evaluating performances are a good way of understanding what went wrong (what, how, why, where and when) and how to improve yourself moving forward. Take full advantage of the performance analysts in the team to aid you in the reflection process.

Determined: push coaches for explanations

We view you as a student of the game so push and challenge coaches to make you into a better player. With a player-centred approach at this football club, the aim is for you to get the most and the best out of practices and match days. Coaches and members of the management team embrace questions because ultimately it is about you becoming the best version of yourself.

Asks searching questions

Always want to learn. Prompt and probe to bring the most out of you and ask questions if there is anything you do not understand.

Socializer: communication

Communicate well with team mates on and off the pitch. Aim to be popular with peers, while this is not an essential characteristic, it is desirable.

Leadership

This football club demands leaders on the football pitch. The captain is not the only leader and all eleven must encourage each other on match day and at practice, to ensure everyone gives the most they possibly can in their performance.

Taking responsibility

Take responsibility for things that may go wrong and learn from everything you experience. Take the initiative to be a leader and grab practice and games by the scruff of the neck, when required.

Adaptable

New pictures, tough conditions, different styles, change of for-mation, new roles and responsibilities are all part of the modern-day game. The modern-day player needs to be able to adapt to any of this that is thrown at them.

OUR PHILOSOPHY ENCOURAGES YOU TO TAKE ADVANTAGE OF DISORGANISATION BY COUNTERING AND PENETRATING WITH SPEED,PRECISION AND PRECISION DIRECTNESS

TEAM PHILOSOPHY

_____

Playing Philosophy

The philosophy that is proposed here is a brief overview of the ideas that as a head coach, I want players and coaches to buy into. It is important to understand that the ideologies and beliefs that make up this philosophy are ever-changing approaches to the game. This develops as the game and rules of the game continue to develop.

Within this philosophy I look to promote a progressive style of football with an ability to adapt to the contextual factors that are in place. This philosophy encourages all players to develop to their full potential in a fun, enjoyable, positive yet highly challenging environment. I intend to do this by implanting non-negotiable foundations such as maintaining a positive attitude in all situations. Being a hard-working team player. Presenting professionalism and honesty in everything that you commit to.

In Possession

Our teams will be playing an intelligent attacking style of football creating overloads around the ball in order to progress into goal scoring opportunities further up the pitch or maintain a patient possession-based game with the aim of getting the ball into attacking areas, with quality as and when the opportunity arises. Wide players will disperse hugging the touchline and make the pitch as wide as possible, strikers will offer height and defenders, including in the goalkeeper, will provide depth. Central players will strategically position themselves vertically and diagonally creating angles to receive the ball.

Players will be encouraged to demonstrate variety, cleverness, courage and calculated risk taking, having taken into consideration the area of the pitch when in possession of the ball.

Counter attacking opportunities will be taken with pace and incorporate 'quick-play' in order to progress and penetrate effectively through the thirds of the pitch, both through central areas and out on the flank positions. Players will be encouraged to take risks in the appropriate areas of the pitch in order to create goal-scoring opportunities.

Transition: OOP – IP

Once possession is recovered players should look to intelligently take advantage of the opposition's disorganization by countering and penetrating with speed, precision and directness. If the opposition are organized or have numbers behind the ball the priority will be to efficiently and effectively adopt a possession-based approach where pass quality, support and movement lead to penetration in the final third, to create goal-scoring opportunities.

Out of Possession

Our out of possession priorities are to prevent the opposition from scoring as well as to regain the ball at the earliest opportunity possible. From here, we will then look to secure the ball before creating goal scoring opportunities. Players are required to be on the front foot looking to engage the ball carrier when it is tactically correct to do so.

Our goal is to set pressing traps to regain the ball from areas that are susceptible for the opposition. These "traps" look at us out-numbering the opponent, preventing them from progressing the ball and making it extremely difficult for them to retain posses-sion. Ultimately, players will have the discipline and understanding of when to press and when to drop while maintaining a compact shape to defend the spaces on the pitch.

Transition: IP – OOP

Once possession is lost, players must energetically apply relent-less pressure to the ball carrier in order to prevent the opposition gaining territory. However, If the ball carrier has time and space on the ball, as a team our psychology switches to one where we look to delay the attack by defending the space in behind and only engaging when we have sufficient numbers who have recovered or the ball carrier gets into a realistic shooting range that presents a threat of a goal being conceded.

Coaching Philosophy

All coaches at the football club are to create a high-performing environment with the values below underpinning everything we do. The non-negotiable values below will create a high performing setting and allow for players to win in the senior phases and fulfil their potential in the youth section.

Non-negotiables

○ Work hard where energy is the minimum players bring to practice and matches
○ Possess a hunger and drive to learn and develop
○ Show respect by playing within the laws and in the spirit of the game

- Be resilient in order to work through adversity
- Within our beliefs, seek to win

Coaches syllabus themes: Attacking

- Making the pitch as big as possible
- Playing out from the back
- Changing speed of play through midfield
- Creating numerical overloads
- Creating and converting chance
- Possession
- Play forward
- Changing tempo
- Counter attacking
- Playing effectively in wide areas
- Finishing

Coaches syllabus themes: Defending

- When to press & when to drop
- Prioritizing the player or space
- 1v1s / 2v1 / 3v2s
- Marking & intercepting
- Possession
- Compactness
- Defending deep
- Defending the long ball
- Defending the counterattack
- Dealing with duels

Playing Environment

The environment that the coach sets needs to be fun, enjoyable, positive yet highly challenging to befit the needs of the players and the wider culture that exists within the club. It is important everyone feels safe in a trusting place where everyone has a voice and everyone's contributions are valued.

This should be an environment that everyone is excited to be a part of, feeling that they can develop as they are continuously challenged in stimulating ways. Going above and beyond is actively encouraged. For example, doing extra skill development sessions before or after practice.

Training Practice

Every coach at every phase in the club must ensure their training practices closely resemble the game they play on the weekend. Football is a directional game in which the goal is situated in central channel of the pitch and this should be reflected in the practice design. Positions and tactical structures are important to the game and where possible should be evident in practices even in small sided games.

Pitch geography is also important in forming fixed objective reference points which players can use to position themselves and where possible they should be incorporated within the practice design. Some artificial markings may also be incorporated to add as a visual aid for key spaces to attack/defend as well as specific positioning within the specific game plan being deployed. Where possible, competition should be incorporated in order to compliment the challenging, fun and energetic environment required in practices.

PRACTICE PLANNING

When planning a practice, it is important to have a focus and to meticulously plan your topic. An example of the level of detail coaches are expected to go into is demonstrated below.

Phase: playing out from the back

Topic: when and how to play our and build up play from the defensive third

NUTRITION

Food is fuel for your body

Keep your body fueled by not skipping meals. Missing meals will cause you to run out of energy and ultimately affect your performance in practice and matches. What you choose not just to eat but also to drink throughout the day influences how you perform so the information in this section is of high importance. What you eat after is equally important for recovery and repair of trauma caused by the physical stress of competition.

What you want out of your foods: Carbohydrates

It is often argued that carbohydrates are the most important source of fuel for the body. Due to this, it is important that 'carbs' play a significant part of each meal, especially breakfast and lunch.

Try to avoid sugar which is the simplest form of carbohydrates because it is not stored in muscle for use later in the day when you are going to need it.

High amounts of sugar will cause your blood sugar levels to increase and your body will overreact by quickly decreasing it to very low levels. (This is when you feel the crash after a sugar high). This will not help you in practice nor on match day. Examples of quality sources of carbohydrates are breads, cereals, porridge, fresh fruit, rice and pastas.

What you want out of your foods: Proteins

Protein should act as a secondary source of fuel but should primarily be consumed post-match. They are essential in repairing muscle tissue after a strenuous workout (practice, lifting, conditioning, games). Examples of quality sources of proteins are lean meat, grilled or baked chicken breast#, turkey breast, tuna, beans, lentils, peanut butter, milk and Greek yoghurt.

What you want out of your foods: fats

Fats provide high sources of energy; they are mostly used when carbohydrates run low in the body. They are usually consumed for long bouts of practice such as fitness sessions and football matches. You will receive plenty of fats from protein sources such as meats, there is no need to supplement fat in your diet.

What you want out of your foods: hydration

It is paramount that you challenge yourself to drink at least 2 litres of water a day. It may help to carry a water bottle around with you to school, college, sixth form, work or around the house. If you are thirsty, you are already dehydrated, however a good indicator as to if you are hydrated is the colour of your urine. This should be a light tint or clear.

Gatorade or Powerade are appropriate after a tough training practice or game. Soda or fizzy drinks, as we best know, do the total opposite of water, so try to avoid these. It is just as significant that you stay away from caffeinated energy drinks and supplements as they are not regulated by the Food and Drug Administration (FDA). Due to the fact they contain high amounts of sugar and caffeine, they contribute a large amount to dehydration, increased heart rate and blood pressure which are all dangerous if consumed prior to an intense practice or game.

Breakfast

Breakfast is an important meal of the day, so it is important you wake up early enough to eat it. This is essentially important before early kick offs. Do not attend the game with an empty stomach as you risk not playing due to lack of energy.

Avoid

Try to avoid what has been listed below, particularly before practice and games. Some of the foods and drinks listed below may have worked for you in the past however it is not sustainable for you for the future and you must aim to look after your body to give yourself the best opportunity of performing

- Hash brown / bacon / sausage / fries
- Eggs (okay occasionally)
- Biscuits
- Waffles
- Pancakes
- Donuts

· Pastries
· Coffee (one small cup is enough – however not before practice)
· Fizzy drinks

Following a guided nutritional plan will help maximize your football career, allow for your football brain to function efficiently and effectively, reduce the risk of injury and aid your recovery from injury.

As well as what you drink and the foods you eat being good for your football career, it will certainly serve to improve your lifestyle. Just because you are fit, it does not mean you are healthy. Have a good diet while exercising regularly to increase the risk of you peaking when required.

MY FITNESS PAL

Tracking your nutrition and activity is very useful and can act as a tool to discipline you through the process. This is a fun, free and effective way to do so.

MyFitnessPal is one of many free nutrition trackers you can easily download on your smartphone app as well as access on the web to help you achieve your goal. Feel free to continue using or accessing your own fitness and nutritional apps if MyFitnessPal is not quite for you.

Step 1

- Log onto www.myfinesspal.com
- Choose to sign up with your Facebook or Sign up with your email address.

Step 2

- Click on Track food (under diet tools) OR food (blue tab).
- Log, breakfast, lunch, dinner and snacks Monday through to Sunday.
- To do this click 'add food' and search for the food you have had, ensure you choose the quantity and serving size after you find your desired choice.

· Once completed at the bottom of the page enter your total water consumption for the day.

Step 3

· Click on 'Track Exercise' (under diet tools) OR exercise (blue tab).
· Choose the 'cardiovascular tab every time, even if you perform strength training.
· To do this click 'add exercise' and search for what you completed.
· Enter in how long you have been exercising for and it will calculate how many calories you have burned.
· At the end of every day, make sure you click on the complete entry button.

*OUR PHILOSOPHY REQUIRES YOU TO DEFEND
EFFECTIVELY & EFFICIENTLY, TO DISPLAY A
CONTROLLED & CALCULATED APPROACH
WHERE EVERY PLAYER CONTRIBUTES & HAS
A CLEAR UNDERSTANDING OF THE TACTICS
BEING USED TO REGAIN POSSESION*

EMBRACING BEING WRONG

———————————————

From our adolescent phase, we are conditioned to want to be right, make no bones about it, we learn that we need to be right. Our guardians applaud us when we do something "well" or better yet answer a question just how they wanted us to. Likewise in school, and yes I am guilty for rewarding dignified behaviour and solid attainment scores. Do we ever really think about suffering caused to those that fail to illicit perfection?

This blunder of coherently being right is a lesson that is re-inforced as we mature. From achieving promotions in the work-place to awarding honours, being right equalled success, whilst being wrong symbolised failure.

The journalist in me continues to flip through newspapers and even these are filled with stories of mistakes made by so-called experts, often followed by the demand that they be punished or sacked or in some way called to account for their errors. If some-thing goes wrong, we seem compelled to look for blame, even if it is difficult to figure out where the fault really lies. Think about when a goal is conceded on the football pitch, someone is attributed with the mistake that led to this. Whatever the wisdom or justice of this mindset in public life, it carries with it an implicit assumption that there is in some way a break from the norm of rightness.

Being wrong is understood as an aberration and I am here to tell you this is wholly inaccurate because we are all wrong. We are always wrong. We are wrong about small, inconsequential things, and we are wrong about big, important matters. We might not want to accept them; we might even try to hide them (from ourselves as well as others). A moment's reflection will remind us that our lives are full of mistakes. We tend to be extremely good at tasks that require quick judgments and actions, but not so good in those situations where reflection is needed.

OUR PHILOSOPHY ARTICULATES IF OPPORTUNITIES TO WIN THE BALL BACK EARLY ARE DENIED, DROP, RECOVER QUICKLY AND ORGANISE A COMPACT DEFENSIVE BLOCK (INCLUDING THE GK) BEHIND THE BALL

A PARENTS' GUIDE TO
INSPIRING PLAYERS

————————————————

Remember: we must all work together as it is commonly proven that children are usually influenced by their own parents' attitudes and behaviors.

Winning versus development

While winning every single football game is pleasant, it is not the single and only measure of development. It is important to understand and appreciate that in our youth phases training practice as well as match days are a time for players to develop their technical, physical, tactical, psychological and social football skills.

This combined with a teaching of the variety of roles and responsibilities of the game will contribute in effectively fulfilling potential. Remember this and refrain from zooming in on simply one focus.

Emotions

As a parent, it is important to the club and for your child that you do not take difficult moments in a game personally. Gifted individuals exist right from the youngest of our youth section right the way through to our senior section. What remains of huge significance is enjoyment above everything. This is so the gifted individuals can continue to thrive and those requiring extra support will be motivated to get there. Ultimately, if your child is enjoying football, they will want to improve and develop further. Research has shown that young children are more interested in playing the game than getting a result.

Feedback

Coaches and members of the management team empathize with parents on how difficult it is to control emotions, especially on match days, as your aim is often to encourage players. However, it is important that in your attempt to do so, players may sometimes be affected by criticism.

Players need positive feedback to feel that they can improve their game and help their team. Instead of highlighting what they have done wrong at practices or in the game, try to phrase your comments constructively and allow the coaches to do their jobs. Children should feel confident that they'll be supported, whether they win or lose.

Too much pressure to win can have a negative effect and put young players off the game altogether. The number of players dropping out of the game is alarming, it is essential we keep players involved in the sport for the right reasons.

The car journey home

Studying individual and team performances and learning how to get the most out of players are what coaches' study all the time. As well as on the coaching course all attend, we run regular CPD workshops to continue developing our knowledge and understanding of the game as well as our players.

Positively support your coaches in the car journey home by making it constructive and reflective. No matter the result, ask questions about how they felt about the game and why. Ask your child what they feel they could have done better and why. This will help them in the future as they will be used to reflecting on their game and finding solutions to improve. Giving players ownership of their learning – mirror our player-centred approach.

Encourage healthy habits

See the nutrition section in this player pack to see the foods to avoid and encourage for your child to eat. Help them eat a balanced diet - including calcium for strong bones, protein for growth and carbohydrates for energy. It is essential that everyday players are drinking plenty of water especially on the day of practice and match days. Not the energy or fizzy drinks, solely water. All players should also ensure they get enough sleep, especially before a match to allow for optimal cognitive focus.

OUR PHILOSOPHY ASKS FOR STRIKERS TO COMBINE WITH EACH OTHER TO CREATE GOAL SCORING OPPORTUNITIES IN AND AROUND THE PENALTY BOX. BE RUTHLESS IN FRONT OF GOAL – BE AGGRESSIVE – DESTROY OPPONENTS

BECOMING A TOP PLAYER

Learning from mistakes

Top players in the game ranging from the Women's Super League (WSL) to the Premier League make just as many errors as anyone else but instead of wasting time thinking about it they pick themselves up, dust themselves down and draw learning out of the unhappy occurrence and move on.

Consistently attending training practice helps you restrict the number of mistakes you make as you go through a continuous learning process.

Recovering from setbacks

Smart learners know that learning can be full of frustration and difficulty, but it doesn't stop them; they learn how to deal with it and don't stay dejected for long.

Attentiveness

Top players know how to concentrate; they focus in their training practice even though there may be other potential distractions going on around them.

Variety in practice

Top players know how to practice in different ways; sometimes they pick out the hard things and knuckle down to work on them and sometimes they focus on the good things about their game and sharpen these skills. Sometimes they work on fluidity and efficiency and polish their performance up and sometimes they try out new things and experiment with trial and error.

Admiration

Top players identify their role models and heroes and spend a lot of time watching how they go about things; they know examining and studying them is a productive use of their time.

Visualization

Top players are good at seeing things in their mind's eye and spend a lot of time imagining themselves performing at a high standard in matches and practice.

Questioning

Top players are not afraid to ask questions, they ask their coach and teammates questions and try out ideas in practice and match days; players who pretend they know it all tend to learn a lot more slowly, if at all.

Rhythms

Top players know how to balance different kinds of learning and they know when to take a break from learning too. They know when to keep pushing for more knowhow and knowledge and when to knuckle down and consolidate what they already know.

Self-teaching

Top players don't wait for the coach to tell them what to do, they develop the ability to design their own learning programs and activities.

Collaboration

Top players know that everyone benefits from teamwork, camaraderie and a generous attitude towards the rest of the squad. So, they know working in fellowship with others is vital to their success.

Going above and beyond

Going above and beyond is actively encouraged. For example, doing extra skill development sessions before or after practice.

ATTITUDE TO LEARNING
REPORT

The learning of our players is an integral part to everything we aspire to achieve at this football club. Players are encouraged to take the accountability in managing their own learning at their own rate, without pressure, this tool is aimed at motivating players week by week.

This action for learning grid (like below) is what coaches will fill out based on both their opinion and the players' opinion on how they feel their training session was. Coaches evaluate training together as a team at the end of training practice and once a month review the action for learning grids to see how individuals are performing. This grid will act as another tool to assist coaches on players' progression.

Format: U12s / 7v7
Player A: Practice: passing and receiving priorities

WWW

Player A executed passes accurately over short distances however there is still work to be done to develop her range over large distances. Player A showed good ability to receive the ball unopposed, in a variety of ways with the weight of pass also differing, this was particularly pleasing.

EBI

Player A has predominantly played this season as a forward and particularly struggled in this practice (as she does in some matches also) to receive the ball with her back to goal. This is an area that needs developing. Some call this 'hold-up play'. While some focus on developing her physical side of the game to improve this part of her game, I do believe it is just as important to develop her receiving techniques and recognizing how best to shield the football.

Home-learning

Watch the following YouTube video to get pictures and to aid learning from home [insert YouTube link].

Extra-curricular

Practice in the garden with a sibling and parent. Setup a rectangle, 10x20 yards in size. A parent feeds the ball into player A who is getting direct pressure from behind by her sibling. Player A shields the ball, turns her sibling and where possible finishes in the goal behind her. Change the area size to increase or decrease the level of difficulty. Add in other plays to set back to, preparing for linking and combining in and around the box for next week's training practice.

YOUTH PHASE; EQUAL PLAYING TIME

———————————————

As consistently echoed in this document, the learning and development of our players is an integral part to everything we aspire to achieve at this football club and equal playing time is essential to this.

Why?

Playing football matches are a vital source of development for youth players. This provides players with the chance to make decisions under a host of pressures. This will not only go a long way with supporting their development as players, but as people also. For example, players can learn on game day how to humbly handle success but also how to deal with inevitable adversity that will come their way. As coaches, we understand that there is an intensity to match day that is almost impossible to recreate in training.

Due to the science, every youth phase of the club will operate a trackable equal playing time record that will be completed by the head coach and sent to coaches on a monthly basis. The learning for all to grasp is that development does not take place in a linear way. A player may excel at seven years of age, but this does not mean they will at ten years of age.

So, it is important every player is given an equal opportunity to succeed. If this does not happen and as the coach you decided your current more advanced players will get more match time, because they simply increase your chance of winning the game they're going to progress at a greater rate than your late developers, who will ultimately get left behind and increase the disparity in ability in your squad now and in the future.

How?

The below example illustrates how we will be keeping record of our youth playing minutes over 80-minute games. This will be viewed and discussed at every monthly coach meeting, with a view to ensure every player never falls below 160 minutes in a four-game cycle.

This is a minimum commitment but the level of playing time is to the discretion of the coach. Coaches and players are encouraged to take advantage of the game-changers on the side line (also known to some as substitutes).

They will be set tasks and challenges which sometime may include low level analysis to contribute to team discussions during intervals.

Player	Minutes vs X Feb. week 1	Minutes vs X Feb. week 2	Minutes vs X Feb. week 3	Minutes vs X Feb. week 4	Total minutes Monthly
A	70	70	70	70	280
B	40	40	60	80	220
C	40	40	40	40	160
D	20	40	20	30	110
E	80	50	60	70	260
F	50	40	60	40	190
G	30	20	40	40	130

OUR PHILOSOPHY REQUIRES PLAYERS IN THE ATTACKING PHASE TO STRETCH OPPONENTS AT EVERY OPPORTUNITY POSSIBLE WITH WIDE PLAYERS OFFERING WIDTH BY HUGGING THE TOUCHLINE, FRONT PLAYERS OFFERING HEIGHT AND PLAYERS AT THE BACK OFFERING DEPTH

PLAYER-CENTRED APPROACH TO COACHING

Adopting a player-centred approach to teaching is what I thoroughly believe will breed success at this football club. Success in understanding our players as people, success in understanding how best to challenge and stretch individuals and ultimately success in absorbing the best out of everyone in training and on game day.

This approach principally means that every individual is at the heart of everything we do. It is imperative that the football environment we create is fun, enjoyable, positive yet highly challenging one. Where the onus is on coaches, staff and parents to provide players with the best opportunity in making the most out of their learning.

This approach for some may be particularly challenging for various reasons. For some they may be used to this style at Ashford over several seasons.

For others they may be coming from an environment which is the total opposite of how the game model is structured here at Ashford Town. For example, we base our training practices under two subheadings. They either fall under clarity in which this is heavily coach led, structured and practices focus solely on teaching the game.

This could be a phase of play training practice. Or they fall under chaos, in which this may often be player led and develop an individual's ability to problem solve such as a small sided possession practice. This player-centred approach could pose challenges to individuals who are used to always being told what to do and for other players they are often given the answer if they continue to struggle. Due to this, some will take a lengthier period to adapt to this style of teaching and learning. A player-centred attitude is not something new, it is a method that has been around for years and utilised in many other sports like hockey and netball.

It is an approach that historically has constraints, as many others also do. For example, this style aims to include player opinion by having representatives from the squads on desired outcomes for the team. However, while this can be very useful for the development and progression of the team, the problem with this is that people have wide ranging experiences and therefore differ in the associations they make. Although most of us have different approaches and opinions on the game, a common consensus will be reached through collaboration that provides the team with the greatest chance of succeeding.

Arguably, the single most difficult task we are facing in the modern-day game is not that players lack the technical or tactical understanding to solve strategic problems within the game. The issue is teaching players to make the right decisions during high levels of stress. Roles and responsibilities have never changed on the football pitch however the pace and intensity of the game very much has. While achieving imminent success is desirable, it is not guaranteed.

Time is needed to create exceptional decision makers, technicians of the ball and leaders on the football pitch. For example, it is my belief that the modern-day defender has evolved to a much quicker, agile and physically sculptured individual who no longer relies on traditional characteristics of solely height, strength and physique. For this reason, we'll adopt to coach not just one style of defending but different modes of play such as; when to press and when and how to defend deep. This way it is giving the players the understanding of the how, where, what and when to defend.

As the management teams are all modern-day students of the game operating a learning-centred way to work, we are under the belief that this approach is crucial to unravelling the confident, proficient and creative player out of the individual. Embrace this approach and become a top player.

OUR PHILOSOPHY REQUIRES GOALKEEPERS TO BE COMFORTABLE IN POSSESSION OF THE FOOTBALL, ESPECIALLY WITH THEIR FEET, IN ORDER FOR THEM TO MEET THE NEEDS OF THE MODERN DAY FOOTBALL PLAYER

FA'S GUIDE TO CONCUSSION

_____

"If in doubt, sit them out"

Footballers who sustain a suspected concussion, either during training or in a game, should immediately be removed from the pitch and not allowed to return until the appropriate treatment has been administered. That is the message at the heart of new guidelines launched by The FA for managing head injuries at all levels of the game.

The advisory guidelines have been designed for those who manage head injuries in professional and grassroots football - from clubs and schools, to parents and doctors.

In summary

- A concussion is an injury to the brain
- While injury to the brain can be fatal, most concussions recover completely with correct management
- All concussions should be regarded as potentially serious and should be managed in accordance with the appropriate guidelines
- Incorrect management of concussion can lead to further injury
- Anyone with any concussion symptoms following a head injury must be removed from playing or training

- Loss of consciousness does not occur in the majority of concussions
- There must be no return to play on the day of any suspected concussion
- Return to education or work must take priority over return to play
- A progressive exercise program that introduces an individual back to sport in a stepwise fashion is recommended after a concussion
- An injury to the cervical spine (neck) may occur at the same time as a concussion and normal principles of cervical spine care should also be followed

These guidelines are intended to give guidance to those managing concussion in football at all levels. Professional and elite level players sometimes have access to an enhanced level of medical care which means that their concussion and their return to play can be managed in a more closely monitored way.

In this situation only, the guidelines for return to play in an enhanced care setting may be followed. These guidelines are based on current evidence and examples of best practice taken from other sports and organizations around the world, including the Rugby Football Union, World Rugby and the Cross-Sports Scottish Sports Concussion Guidance. Advice has also been sought from The FA's Expert Panel on Concussion and Head Injury in Football.

The guidelines are in line with the Consensus Statement on Concussion in Sport issued by the Fifth International Conference on Concussion in Sport, Berlin 2016. This version has been updated as of August 2019.

While these guidelines aim to reflect 'best practice', all accept that there is a current lack of evidence in respect to their effectiveness in preventing long-term harm. The FA will continue to monitor research and consensus in the area of concussion and update these guidelines accordingly.

[thefa.com]

TROPHIES AND CHAMPIONSHIPS

_____

Brentford Women FC

Greater London Women's Football League:

Division 2: 2012/13

Division 1: 2013/14

GLWFL Russell Cup: 2012/13, 2013/14

Capital Cup Junior: 2013/14

Ashford Town (Middlesex) FC Women

Greater London Women's Football League:

Division 3: 2015/16

Division 2: 2016/17

Premier: 2018/19

Sue Sharples Memorial Trophy: 2015/16

GLWFL Trophy: 2016/17, 2017/18

Capital Cup Junior: 2016/17

Capital Cup Intermediate: 2018/19

London & South East Regionals Premier: 2021/22

Capital Cup Senior: 2021/22

Combined Counties Midweek Trophy: 2021/22

SEASON 2015/16 - GLWFL DIVISION 3 (SOUTH)

06/09/15 - Old Actonians 1- 11 Ashford Town (Middlesex) FC Women

Lineup - L Restel, J Harker, L Huse, A Cheatley, V James (captain), A Luzar, L Neufville, P Pantlin, K Peart, C Samuels, I Smith

13/09/15 - Ashford Town (Middlesex) FC Women 8-3 Putney Vale

Lineup - L Restel, C McGregor, J Boyd, T Prior, L Huse, L Neufville, A O'Sullivan, C Benham, C Richardson, V James (captain), A Cheatley

20/09/15 - Club Langley 0-18 Ashford Town (Middlesex) FC Women

Lineup - L Restel, J Harker, L Huse, A Cheatley, V James (captain), A Luzar, L Neufville, P Pantlin, K Peart, C Samuels, I Smith

27/09/15 - Ashford Town (Middlesex) FC Women 13-0 London Phoenix

Lineup - L Restel, A Luzar, R Thurlow, J Boyd, K Peart, L Neufville, V James (captain), C Samuels, I Smith, P Pantilin, A Cheatley

04/10/15 - Ashford Town (Middlesex) FC Women 12-0 Old Actonians

Lineup - L Restel, A Luzar, J Harker, J Boyd, L Huse, V James (captain), C Samuels, L Neufville, I Smith, R Thurlow, A Cheatley

11/10/15 - Hammersmith Starz 5-0 Ashford Town (Middlesex) FC Women

Lineup - L Restel, F Larsson, A Luzar, P Pantlin, L Huse, C Benham, C Samuels, V James (captain), I Smith, L Neufville, A Cheatley

25/10/15 - Colne Valley Reserves 5-2 Ashford Town (Middlesex) FC Women

Lineup - L Restel, F Larsson, A Luzar, P Pantlin, L Huse, C Benham, C Samuels, V James (captain), I Smith, L Neufville, A Cheatley

13/11/15 - Ashford Town (Middlesex) FC Women 6-0 Orpington Ladies

Lineup - L Easton, C McGregor, A Luzar, F Larsson, R Thurlow, A O'Sullivan, T Prior, V James (captain), C Benham, P Pantlin, A Cheatley

06/12/15 - Putney Vale 1-4 Ashford Town (Middlesex) FC Women

Lineup - L Restel, C McGregor, J Boyd, T Prior, L Huse, L Neufville, A O'Sullivan, C Benham, C Richardson, V James (captain), A Cheatley

13/12/15 - Ashford Town (Middlesex) FC Women 5-0 Club Langley

Lineup - L Restel, L Huse, C McGregor, P Pantlin, J Boyd, F Larsson, I Smith, V James (captain), L Neufville, A Cheatley

17/01/16 - Orpington Ladies 0-2 Ashford Town (Middlesex) FC Women*

24/01/16 - London Phoenix 1-7 Ashford Town (Middlesex) FC Women

Lineup - L Restel, C McGregor, L Huse, A Luzar (captain), J Boyd, T Prior, C Samuels, A O'Sullivan, I Smith, C Benham, A Cheatley

07/02/16 - Ashford Town (Middlesex) FC Women 3-3 Hammersmith Smith Starz

Lineup - L Restel, C McGregor F Larsson, A Luzar, B Sheehan, T Prior, V James(captain), C Samuels, L Neufville, A Cheatley, C Benham

* Fixtures were rewarded as walkover victories.

SEASON 2016/17 - GLWFL DIVISION 2 (SOUTH)

04/09/16 - Ashford Town (Middlesex) FC Women 3-1 Surrey Eagles

Lineup - L Restel, L Huse, C Benham, T Prior, J Boyd, T Frost, C Samuels, V James (captain), I Smith, S Belworthy, A Cheatley

Scorers - S Belworthy (30'), A Cheatley (40'), I Smith (53')

11/09/16 - Ashford Town (Middlesex) FC Women 7-1 Balham Panthers

Lineup - L Restel, L Huse, N Jacobs, L Neufville, T Prior, T Frost, C Samuels (captain), I Smith, S Belworthy, H Isaacs, A Cheatley

Scorers - A Cheatley (11'), (17'), (32'), (47'), (87'), H Isaacs (58'), L Neufville (71')

25/09/16 - Ashford Town (Middlesex) FC Women 6-2 Carshalton Athletic Development

Lineup - L Restel, A Luzar, N Jacobs, C Benham, J Boyd, L Neufville, T Frost, L Richardson, V James (captain), I Smith, A Cheatley

Scorers - A Cheatley (5'), (35'), (46'), L Neufville (16'), T Frost (75'), V James (88')

02/10/16 - Crystal Palace Reserves 1-6 Ashford Town (Middlesex) FC Women

Lineup - L Restel, A Luzar, N Jacobs, C Benham, J Boyd, L Neufville, T Frost, S Phillips-Hines, V James (captain), H Isaacs, A Cheatley

Scorers - H Isaacs (18'), A Cheatley (28'), (60'), L Neufville (42'), (85'), S Phillips-Hines (54')

09/10/16 - Putney Vale 1-1 Ashford Town (Middlesex) FC Women

Lineup - L Restel, A Luzar, N Jacobs, C Benham, J Boyd, L Neufville, L Richardson, S Phillips-Hines, V James (captain), H Isaacs, A Cheatley

Scorer - C Benham (84')

06/11/16 - Ashford Town (Middlesex) FC Women 4-1 Godalming Town

Lineup - L Restel, L Neufville, N Jacobs, T Mills, J Boyd, I Smith, C Benham, V James (captain), C Samuels, H Isaacs, A Cheatley

Scorers - A Cheatley (30'), (66'), (83'), C Samuels (43')

13/11/16 - Ashford Town (Middlesex) FC Women 14-1 Clapham United

Lineup - L Restel, B Sheehan, L Huse, T Mills, J Boyd, I Smith, C Benham, V James (captain), H Isaacs, L Neufville, A Cheatley

Scorers - A Cheatley (2'), (15'), (30'), (34'), (46'), (77'), I Smith (27'), (48'), (53'), V James (22'), (50'), L Neufville (12'), (84'), (90')

20/11/16 - Larkspur Rovers 0-10 Ashford Town (Middlesex) FC Women

Lineup - A Luzar, B Sheehan, L Huse, L Richardson, J Boyd, I Smith, C Benham, V James (captain), H Isaacs, L Neufville, A Cheatley

Scorers - A Cheatley (1'), (10'), (17'), (30'), (33'), L Neufville (52'), (61'), (67'), I Smith (23'), (24')

27/11/16 - Clapham United Reserves 1-3 Ashford Town (Middlesex) FC Women

Lineup - L Richardson, B Sheehan, L Huse, A Luzar, J Boyd, I Smith, C Benham, V James (captain), L Neufville, S Belworthy, A Cheatley

Scorers - A Cheatley (19'), (86'), C Benham (74')

0412/16 - Colne Valley Reserves 1-1 Ashford Town (Middlesex) FC Women

Lineup - L Restel, L Richardson, L Huse, T Mills, A Luzar, J Boyd, I Smith, C Benham, V James (captain), H Isaacs, A Cheatley

Scorer - A Cheatley (63')

29/01/17 - Ashford Town (Middlesex) FC Women 9-0 Colne Valley Reserves

Lineup - L Restel, J Boyd, B Sheehan, N Jacobs, L Huse, V James (captain), S Phillips-Hines, C Benham, H Isaacs, L Neufville, S Belworthy

Scorers - H Isaacs (1'), (35'), L Neufville (12'), (64'), S Belworthy (15'), (42'), (58'), C Benham (70'), (90'), S Phillips-Hines (90')

05/02/17 - Greenhouse Sports 1-8 Ashford Town (Middlesex) FC Women

Lineup - L Restel, J Boyd, A Luzar, L Huse, N Jacobs, V James (captain), C Benham, S Phillips-Hines, L Neufville, S Belworthy, A Cheatley

Scorers - C Benham (30'), S Belworthy (32'), (40'), (51'), (77'), (85'), L Neufville (56'), (63')

12/02/17 - Ashford Town (Middlesex) FC Women 13-0 Putney Vale

Lineup - A Luzar, J Boyd, N Jacobs, L Huse, B Sheehan, C Benham, V James (captain), S Phillips-Hines, H Isaacs, S Belworthy, L Neufville

Scorers - H Isaacs (8'), (30'), (61'), (69'), (81'), V James (12'),S Belworthy (15'), (42'), (60'), (87'), C Benham (24'), S Phillips-Hines (52'), L Neufville (74')

26/02/17 - Balham Panthers 0-4 Ashford Town (Middlesex) FC Women

Lineup - L Restel, B Sheehan, L Huse, N Jacobs, J Boyd, V James (captain), S Phillips-Hines, C Benham, H Isaacs, L Neufville, S Belworthy

Scorers - S Belworthy (32'), H Isaacs (35'),V James (40'),L Neufville (86')

12/03/17 - Ashford Town (Middlesex) FC Women 10-1 Crystal Palace Reserves

Lineup - L Restel, A Luzer, L Huse, N Jacobs, B Sheehan, V James (captain), S Phillips-Hines, L Richardson, H Isaacs, L Neufville, S Belworthy

Scorers - H Isaacs (5'), (7'), L Neufville (9'), (58'), (65'), S Belworthy (12'), (40'), (68'), L Richardson (52'), L Huse (55')

26/03/17 - Carshalton Athletic Development 2-7 Ashford Town (Middlesex) FC Women

Lineup - L Restel, J Densu, L Huse, B Sheehan, J Boyd, V James (captain), T Mills, N Jacobs, L Richardson, L Neufville, S Belworthy

Scorers - N Jacobs (5'), L Neufville (15'), (45'), (70'), S Belworthy (25'), (75'), L Richardson (31')

02/04/17 - Godalming Town 1-1 Ashford Town (Middlesex) FC Women

Lineup - L Restel, A Luzar, L Huse, N Jacobs, J Boyd, V James (captain), H Noonan, C Benham, L Neufville, H Isaacs, S Belworthy

Scorer - S Belworthy (90')

23/04/17 - Surrey Eagles 1-14 Ashford Town (Middlesex) FC Women

Lineup - L Restel, A Luzar, L Huse, N Jacobs, J Boyd, V James (captain), T Mills, L Richardson, B Sheehan, L Neufville, S Belworthy

Scorers - L Richardson (13'), (55'), (44'), (85'), L Neufville (15'), (35'), (61'), (75'), (86'), S Belworthy (45'), (53'), (67'), A Luzar (79'), V James (89')

30/04/17 - Ashford Town (Middlesex) FC Women 2-0 Greenhouse Sports*

* Fixtures were rewarded as walkover victories.

24/09/17 - Ashford Town (Middlesex) FC Women 6-1 Luton Town Development

Lineup - L Restel, M Bone, L Huse, C Benham, B Sheehan, V James (captain), T Mills, L Richardson, B Sheehan, L Neufville, S Belworthy

Scorers - A Cheatley (10'), (45'), L Neufville (20'), (42'), S Belworthy (38'), S Burgess (45')

01/10/17 - Bromley FC 0-3 Ashford Town (Middlesex) FC Women

Lineup - C Baker, M Bone, H Pearson, N Jacobs, B Sheehan, C Benham, V James (captain), R Fisher, H Isaacs, B Sheehan, L Neufville, S Belworthy

Scorers - L Neufville(25'), H Isaacs (35'), V James (65' Pen)

22/10/17 - Ashford Town (Middlesex) FC Women 6-3 Hampton & Richmond Borough

Lineup - L Restel, M Bone, J Boyd, C Baker, L Huse, V James (captain), R Fisher, C Benham, H Isaacs, L Neufville, A Cheatley

Scorers - L Neufville (8'), (79'), A Cheatley (11'), (70'), H Isaacs (30'), C Benham (64')

29/10/17 - Ashford Town (Middlesex) FC Women 5-0 Clapham United

Lineup - L Restel, C Baker, L Huse (captain), N Jacobs, B Sheehan, H Pearson, R Fisher, S Phillips-Hines, S Belworthy, L Neufville, A Cheatley

Scorers - S Phillips-Hines (23'), A Cheatley (34'), (56'), (65'), H Isaacs (75')

05/11/17 - Kingstonian 1-4 Ashford Town (Middlesex) FC Women

Lineup - S Burgess, B Sheehan, C Baker, L Huse, N Jacobs, V James (captain), C Samuels, C Benham, L Neufville, H Isaacs, A Cheatley

Scorers - L Neufville (25'), A Cheatley (49'), (56'), M Bone (79')

26/11/17 - Clapham United 1-2 Ashford Town (Middlesex) FC Women

Lineup - L Restel, C Baker, L Huse, M Bone, B Sheehan, V James (captain), H Pearson, C Benham, H Isaacs, L Neufville, A Cheatley

Scorers - A Cheatley (71'), C Benham (79')

03/12/17 - Ashford Town (Middlesex) FC Women 4-0 Bromley FC

Lineup - L Restel, C Baker, L Huse, M Bone, N Jacobs, V James (captain), H Pearson, S Phillips-Hines, L Thornton, L Neufville, C Benham

Scorers - V James (13'), L Neufville (27'), S Phillips-Hines (63'), H Pearson (75')

07/01/18 - Hampton & Richmond Borough 3-2 Ashford Town (Middlesex) FC Women

Lineup - L Restel, C Baker, L Huse, M Bone, N Jacobs, V James (captain), H Pearson, S Burgess, H Isaacs, L Neufville, C Benham

Scorers - V James (25'),H Isaacs (40')

28/01/18 - Ashford Town (Middlesex) FC Women 2-2 Brentford WFC

Lineup - L Restel, B Sheehan, C Baker, L Huse, N Jacobs, V James (captain), H Pearson, H Isaacs, L Neufville, C Benham, A Cheatley

Scorers - C Benham (30'), L Neufville (80')

11/02/18 - Ashford Town (Middlesex) FC Women 2-2 Godalming Town

Lineup - L Restel, B Sheehan, M Bone, C Baker, L Huse, V James (captain), H Pearson, H Isaacs, L Neufville, C Benham, A Cheatley

Scorers - L Neufville (35'), H Isaacs (60')

18/02/18 - Ashford Town (Middlesex) FC Women 7-0 Colne Valley

Lineup - L Restel, M Bone, C Baker, L Huse (captain), S Burgess, H Pearson, B Sheehan, Ella Hill, L Neufville, C Benham, A Cheatley

Scorers - L Neufville (20'), (30'), (55'), (75'), A Cheatley (25'), V James (65'), E Hill (70')

25/02/18 - New London Lionesses 3-1 Ashford Town (Middlesex) FC Women

Lineup - L Restel, M Bone, C Baker, L Huse, J Boyd, H Pearson, V James (captain), B Sheehan, L Neufville, C Benham, A Cheatley

Scorer - B Sheehan (45')

11/03/18 - Ashford Town (Middlesex) FC Women 3-0 Kingstonian

Lineup - L Restel, M Bone, N Jacobs, L Huse, S Burgess, H Pearson, V James (captain), H Isaacs, L Neufville, C Benham, A Cheatley

Scorers - A Cheatley (65'), (70'), L Thornton (86')

03/04/18 - Godalming Town 2-1 Ashford Town (Middlesex) FC Women

Lineup - S Burgess, M Bone, N Jacobs, L Huse (captain), J Boyd, H Pearson, R Fisher, H Isaacs, L Neufville, C Benham, A Cheatley

Scorer - A Cheatley (81')

15/04/18 - Brentford WFC 5-8 Ashford Town (Middlesex) FC Women

Lineup - L Restel, M Bone, N Jacobs, L Huse (captain), S Burgess, H Pearson, C Benham, H Isaacs, R Fisher, L Neufville, A Cheatley

Scorers - L Neufville (32'), (39'), (84'), A Cheatley (41'), (58'), L Huse (44'), (76' Pen), C Benham (60')

29/04/18 - Luon Town Development 0-4 Ashford Town (Middlesex) FC Women

Lineup - L Restel, M Bone, N Jacobs, L Huse (captain), S Burgess, H Pearson, C Benham, H Isaacs, R Fisher, L Neufville, A Cheatley

Scorers - H Isaacs (28'), (71'), A Cheatley (35'), (60')

06/05/18 - Ashford Town (Middlesex) FC Women 1-2 New London Lionesses

Lineup - L Restel, M Bone, N Jacobs, L Huse (captain), C Baker, H Pearson, C Benham, H Isaacs, R Fisher, L Neufville, L Thornton

Scorer - L Thornton (90')

09/09/18 - Ashford Town (Middlesex) FC Women 10-0 Colne Valley

Lineup - S Burgess, R French, C Baker, L Huse, H Freeman, H Pearson, C Benham (captain), A Down, H Isaacs, A Cheatley, L Neufville

Scorers - H Isaacs (1'), A Cheatley (7'), (18'), (51'), (51'), (57'), (60'), (80'), L Huse (70'), L Neufville (75'), D Johnson (85')

16/09/18 - Tottenham Hotspur Development 2-7 Ashford Town (Middlesex) FC Women

Lineup - S Burgess, B Sheehan, R French, L Huse, H Freeman, H Pearson, C Benham (captain), A Down, H Isaacs, A Cheatley, L Neufville

Scorers - H Freeman (1'), A Cheatley (2'), L Neufville (25'), C Benham (31'), R Fisher (45'), A Down (65'), L Huse (88')

30/09/18 - Regents Park 1-7 Ashford Town (Middlesex) FC Women

Lineup - S Burgess, N Peters, R French, L Huse, S Treadaway, H Pearson, C Benham (captain), A Down, B Sheehan, H Isaacs, L Neufville

Scorers - B Sheehan (35'), L Neufville (42'), C Benham (50'), D Johnson (55'), N Peters (70'), R French (75'), L Huse (10')

14/10/18 - Ashford Town (Middlesex) FC Women 12-1 Watford Ladies Development

Lineup - L Restel, M Bone, C Baker, L Huse, S Treadaway, C Benham (captain), A Down, R French, S Carpenter, L Neufville, A Cheatley

Scorers - A Cheatley (7'), (49'), (52'), (55'), L Neufville (13'), (82'),L Huse (17'), R French (33'), A Down (36'), S Carpenter (68'), (71'), S Smith (28' OG)

28/10/18 - Ashford Town (Middlesex) FC Women 5-1 Victoire Ladies

Lineup - L Restel, N Peters, B Sheehan, L Huse (captain), S Treadaway, H Pearson, A Down, R French, S Carpenter, L Neufville, A Cheatley

Scorers - A Cheatley (13' Pen), (54'), (75'), A Down (17'), D Johnson (66')

04/11/18 - Ashford Town (Middlesex) FC Women 5-1 Hackney Women

Lineup - S Burgess, J Boyd, M Bone, L Huse (captain), H Freeman, H Pearson, B Keeping, S Carpenter, R French, L Nefuville, A Cheatley

Scorers - R French (20'), L Neufville (25'), L Huse (29' Pen), A Cheatley (48'),P Head (75')

25/11/18 - Godalming Town 1-1 Ashford Town (Middlesex) FC Women

Lineup - L Restel, L Huse, S Treadaway, N Peters, R French, H Pearson, C Benham (captain), H Isaacs, P Head, L Neufville, A Cheatley

Scorer - A Cheatley (58')

02/12/18 - New London Lionesses 1-4 Ashford Town (Middlesex) FC Women

Lineup - S Burgess, N Peters, M Bone, L Huse (captain), S Treadaway, H Pearson, L Neufville, S Carpenter, H Isaacs, R French, A Cheatley

Scorers - R French (25'), L Neufville (33'), (62'), L Huse (55')

09/12/18 - Colne Valley 1-4 Ashford Town (Middlesex) FC Women

Lineup - G Perkis, M Bone, L Huse (captain), S Treadaway, C Baker, G Goodwin, H Pearson, A Down, L Neufville, H Isaacs, A Cheatley

Scorers - A Down (66'), A Cheatley (70'), (78'), (86')

06/01/19 - Ashford Town (Middlesex) FC Women 3-2 Tottenham Hotspur Development

Lineup - G Perkis, L Huse, S Treadaway, N Peters, C Baker, H Pearson, A Down, L Neufville, P Head, R French, A Cheatley

Scorers - R French (20'), A Cheatley (44'), (44'), L Huse (72')

24/02/19 - Hackney Women 2-2 Ashford Town (Middlesex) FC Women

Lineup - G Perkis, M Bone, L Huse, S Treadaway, G Goodwin, H Pearson, A Down, C Benham (captain), L Neufville, H Isaacs, A Cheatley

Scorers - A Cheatley (18'), A Down (90')

03/03/19 - Victoire Ladies 2-0 Ashford Town (Middlesex) FC Women *

17/03/19 - Ashford Town (Middlesex) FC Women 7-1 Regents Park

Lineup - G Perkis, N Peters, L Huse, M DeLuca, C Baker, H Pearson, A Down, C Benham (captain), P Head, L Neufville, H Isaacs

Scorers - L Neufville (1'), (5'), (35'), (40'), (52'), (74'), H Isaacs (48')

31/03/19 - Watford Ladies Development 2-9 Ashford Town (Middlesex) FC Women

Lineup - G Perkis, N Peters, L Huse, M DeLuca, C Baker, H Pearson, A Down, C Benham (captain), P Head, L Neufville, S Mann

Scorers - L Neufville (27'), (43'), (47'), A Down (36'), (81'), A Cheatley (71'), (78'), (80') C Benham (54')

05/05/19 - Ashford Town (Middlesex) FC Women 3-2 Godalming Town

Lineup - G Perkis, M Bone, L Huse, S Treadaway, C Baker, H Pearson, A Down, C Benham (captain), H Isaacs, L Neufville, A Cheatley

Scorers - A Cheatley (10'), (66'), C Benham (38')

12/05/19 - Ashford Town (Middlesex) FC Women 1-3 New London Lionesses

Lineup - G Perkis, N Peters, L Huse (captain), S Treadaway, C Baker, H Pearson, A Down, L Neufville, E Kriebel, L Neufville, M Adcock

Scorer - L Neufville (83')

SEASON 2019/20 - L&SERWFL PREMIER DIVISION

25/08/19 - Ashford Town (Middlesex) FC Women 3-2 Whyteleafe Women

Lineup - G Perkis, N Peters, D Lawrence, C Baker, L Potter, H Symons, H Pearson (captain), A Down, H Isaacs, E Kriebel, L Neufville

Scorers - H Pearson (31'), L Neufville (61'), C Baker (83')

08/09/19 - Dartford Women 5-2 Ashford Town (Middlesex) FC Women

Lineup - G Perkis, J Berggren, L Huse (captain), A Harte, C Baker, H Symons, C Benham, A Down, P Head, J Johnson, L Neufville

Scorers - P Head (25'), (28')

15/09/19 - Ashford Town (Middlesex) FC Women 5-1 Eastbourne Town

Lineup - G Perkis, N Peters, L Huse (captain), D Lawrence, C Baker, H Symons, H Pearson, A Down, J Johnson, L Neufville, A Cheatley

Scorers - C Baker (25'), A Cheatley (36'), L Huse (65'), L Neufville (73'), (85')

06/10/19 - Ashford Town (Middlesex) FC Women 1-1 Dulwich Hamlet

Lineup - G Perkis, N Peters, L Huse (captain), A Harte, L Potter, H Symons, C Benham, A Down, J Johnson, P Head, L Neufville

Scorer - P Head (35')

20/10/19 - Ashford Town (Middlesex) FC Women 1-2 Denham United

Lineup - G Perkis, N Peters, L Huse (captain), H Pearson, L Potter, H Symons, C Benham, A Down, J Johnson, L Neufville, A Cheatley

Scorer - A Cheatley (8')

27/10/19 - Dulwich Hamlet 2-0 Ashford Town (Middlesex) FC Women

Lineup - L Restel, N Peters, L Huse (captain), A Harte, L Potter, H Pearson, A Down, J Johnson, L Neufville, A Cheatley, J Wilson

10/11/19 - Denham United 1-2 Ashford Town (Middlesex) FC Women

Lineup - G Perkis, N Peters, L Huse (captain), H Pearson, L Potter, C Benham, A Down, J Johnson, L Neufville, A Cheatley, J Wilson

Scorers - A Cheatley (55'), (71')

08/12/19 - Aylesford Ladies 1-6 Ashford Town (Middlesex) FC Women

Lineup - G Perkis, N Peters, L Huse (captain), C Baker, L Potter, C Benham, A Down, J Johnson, H Pearson, L Neufville, A Cheatley

Scorers - A Down (15'), L Huse (35'), A Cheatley (71'), (78'), (80'), (81')

19/01/20 - Eastbourne Town 1-3 Ashford Town (Middlesex) FC Women

Lineup - G Perkis, J Johnson, L Huse (captain), C Baker, L Potter, C Farrell, A Down, R Linton, H Symons, P Head, A Cheatley

Scorers - R Linton (26'), A Cheatley (45'), P Head (49')

26/01/20 - Fulham Women 3-4 Ashford Town (Middlesex) FC Women

Lineup - G Perkis, N Peters, L Huse (captain), C Baker, L Potter, A Down, J Johnson, H Pearson, C Farrell, L Neufville, R Linton

Scorers - L Neufville (11'), A Down (49' Pen), R Linton (53'), N Peters (85')

08/03/20 - Ashford Town (Middlesex) FC Women 5-5 Fulham Women

Lineup - G Perkis, N Peters, A Harte, H Pearson, L Potter, A Down (captain), C Benahm, J Johnson, H Symons, A Cheatley, L Neufville

Scorers - A Cheatley (8'), (57'), (83'), C Benham (66'), L Neufville (80')

SEASON 2020/21 - L&SERWFL PREMIER DIVISION

———————————

13/09/20 - Dartford Women 2-0 Ashford Town (Middlesex) FC Women

Lineup - G Perkis, L Huse, A Kinnane, K Spencer, L Potter, C Benahm, A Down (captain), H Pearson, R Sitarz, A Cheatley, L Neufville

27/09/20 - Ashford Town (Middlesex) FC Women 3-2 Eastbourne Town

Lineup - G Perkis, L Huse, A Kinnane, K Peart, L Potter, C Benahm, A Down (captain), J Johnson, H Pearson, A Cheatley, L Neufville

Scorers - A Down (30'), C Benham (65'), A Cheatley (86')

11/10/20 - Aylesford Ladies 3-8 Ashford Town (Middlesex) FC Women

Lineup - G Perkis, L Huse, A Kinnane, K Peart, L Potter, C Benahm, A Down (captain), J Johnson, H Pearson, A Cheatley, L Neufville

Scorers - J Johnson (15'), A Kinnane (18'), (70'), A Cheatley (38'), (65'), L Neufville (49'), (80'), H Nebbitt (58')

01/11/20 - Whyteleafe Women 3-5 Ashford Town (Middlesex) FC Women

Lineup - G Perkis, L Huse, A Kinnane, L Potter, A Down (captain), V James, J Johnson, P Head, H Pearson, R Sitarz, A Cheatley

Scorers - A Cheatley (30'), (41'), (83'), J Johnson (61'), A Kinnane (80')

18//04/21 - Saltdean United 1-3 Ashford Town (Middlesex) FC Women **

Scorers - A Cheatley (2'), J Wilson (12'), K Peart (48')

25/04/21 - Eastbourne Town 3-5 Ashford Town (Middlesex) FC Women **

Scorers - A Cheatley (25'), P Head (35'), A Down (40'), (65'), L Potter (48')

02/05/21 - Dartford Women 1-3 Ashford Town (Middlesex) FC Women **

Scorers - A Cheatley (20'), J Johnson (25'), C Farrell (65')

09/05/21 - QPR Women 1-8 Ashford Town (Middlesex) FC Women **

Scorers - J Johnson (8'), N Douglas (18'), (29'), (75'), K Peart (35'),A Cheatley (49'), (57'),H Pearson (81')

23/05/21 - Dulwich Hamlet 2-3 Ashford Town (Middlesex) FC Women **

Scorers - C Farrell (30'), A Kinnane (50'), A Cheatley (90')

** Spring series competition.

.

SEASON 2021/22 - L&SERWFL PREMIER DIVISION

22/08/21 - Ashford Town (Middlesex) FC Women 9-1 Millwall Lionesses

Lineup - S Shults, A Kinnane, F Cotter, K Peart, C Baker, A Holdcroft, A Down (captain), H Pearson, J Johnson, A Cheatley, L Neufville

Scorers - A Cheatley (20'), (76'), L Neufville (27'), (36'), (40'), (67'), A Down (44'), (49' Pen), P Head (89')

29/08/21 - Ashford Town (Middlesex) FC Women 8-1 Aylesford Ladies

Lineup - S Shults, A Kinnane, F Cotter, L Potter, C Baker, M McGarvey, A Down (captain), H Pearson, J Johnson, A Cheatley, L Neufville

Scorers - A Kinnane (20'), (78'), (94'), A Cheatley (68'), (88'), L Neufville (73'), A Down (78'), (80'), (89'), (94')

05/09/21 - Saltdean United 2-5 Ashford Town (Middlesex) FC Women

Lineup - G Perkis, K Peart, F Cotter, L Huse, C Baker, A Kinnane, A Down (captain), L Potter, J Johnson, A Cheatley, L Neufville

Scorers - K Peart (15'), J Johnson (22'), A Down (30'), A Cheatley (42'), (60')

12/09/21 - Ashford Town (Middlesex) FC Women 4-2 New London Lionesses

Lineup - S Shults, M McGarvey, E Clarabut, C Baker, C Farrell, A Kinnane, A Down (captain), L Potter, J Johnson, A Cheatley, L Neufville

Scorers - A Down (22'), A Cheatley (45'), (90'), C Farrell (86')

19/09/21 - Dartford Women 2-3 Ashford Town (Middlesex) FC Women

Lineup - S Shults, L Potter, A Kinnane, E Clarabut, C Baker, A Down (captain), C Farrell, J Johnson, M McGarvey, A Cheatley, L Neufville

Scorers - A Cheatley (10'), (69'), (85')

26/09/21 - Ashford Town (Middlesex) FC Women 8-0 Worthing Women

Lineup - S Shults, C Baker, A Kinnane, E Clarabut, A Down (captain), C Farrell, J Johnson, R Sitarz, M McGarvey, A Cheatley, L Neufville

Scorers - A Cheatley (10'), (49'), (51'), (62'), L Neufville (24'), (35'), (67'), (74')

17/10/21 - Dulwich Hamlet 1-1 Ashford Town (Middlesex) FC Women

Lineup - S Shults, C Baker, A Kinnane, E Clarabut, A Down (captain), C Farrell, J Johnson, R Sitarz, K Peart, A Cheatley, L Neufville

Scorer - A Kinnane (67')

07/11/21 - Ashford Town (Middlesex) FC Women 4-1 Denham United

Lineup - S Shults, F Cotter, A Kinnane, E Clarabut, A Down (captain), C Farrell, J Johnson, R Sitarz, K Peart, A Cheatley, L Neufville

Scorers - A Cheatley (20'), (63'), R Sitarz (52'), A Down (84')

09/01/22 - Denham United 1-6 Ashford Town (Middlesex) FC Women

Lineup - S Shults, A Kinnane, E Clarabut, J Johnson, A Down (captain), C Farrell, J Hoesli-Atkins, R Sitarz, R Linton, A Cheatley, L Neufville

Scorers - L Neufville (24'), A Cheatley (29'), R Linton (40'), R Sitarz (55'), A Down (66'), J Johnson (80')

16/01/22 - Ashford Town (Middlesex) FC Women 1-1 Fulham Women

Lineup - S Shults, A Kinnane, E Clarabut, J Johnson, A Down (captain), C Farrell, J Hoesli-Atkins, R Sitarz, R Linton, A Cheatley, L Neufville

Scorers - A Down (65' Pen)

23/01/22 - Millwall Lionesses 0-4 Ashford Town (Middlesex) FC Women

Lineup - S Shults, L Huse, A Kinnane, E Clarabut, J Johnson, A Down (captain), C Farrell, K Peart, R Sitarz, A Cheatley, L Neufville

Scorers - A Down (25'), A Cheatley (35'), R Linton (60'), L Neufville (74')

30/01/22 - Ashford Town (Middlesex) FC Women 2-0 Dartford Women

Lineup - S Shults (captain), L Huse, C Baker, E Clarabut, C Farrell, J Hoesli-Atkins, K Peart, R Sitarz, R Linton, A Cheatley, L Neufville

Scorers - L Huse (75' Pen), R Linton (85')

13/02/22 - Ashford Town (Middlesex) FC Women 3-0 Saltdean United

Lineup - S Shults, A Kinnane, E Clarabut, J Johnson, A Down (captain), C Farrell, K Peart, R Sitarz, R Linton, A Cheatley, L Neufville

Scorers - K Peart (30'), (55'), A Down (44' Pen)

13/03/22 - New London Lionesses 1-6 Ashford Town (Middlesex) FC Women

Lineup - S Shults, A Kinnane, E Clarabut, L Huse, J Hoseli-Atkins, A Down (captain), K Peart, R Sitarz, R Linton, A Cheatley, L Neufville

Scorers - L Neufville (26'), (79'), R Sitarz (65'), A Cheatley (67'), C Farrell (71'), C Bisson (80')

27/03/22 - Ashford Town (Middlesex) FC Women 2-0 Dulwich Hamlet Ladies

Lineup - S Shults, A Kinnane, E Clarabut, C Baker, C Farrell, A Down (captain), K Peart, R Linton, J Johnson, A Cheatley, L Neufville

Scorers - L Neufville (41'), A Cheatley (70')

03/03/22 - Worthing Women 0-5 Ashford Town (Middlesex) FC Women

Lineup - S Shults, A Kinnane, J Johnson, E Clarabut, H Pearson, J Hoesli-Atkins, A Down (captain), K Peart, R Linton, A Cheatley, L Neufville

Scorers - K Peart (2'), L Neufville (33'), (86'), A Down (59'), A Cheatley (80')

10/04/22 - Whyteleafe 0-10 Ashford Town (Middlesex) FC Women

Lineup - S Shults, A Kinnane, J Johnson, E Clarabut, L Huse, C Farrell, A Down (captain), K Peart, R Linton, A Cheatley, L Neufville

Scorers - R Linton (4'), (55'), J Johnson (26'), K Peart (35'), A Cheatley (50'), (80'), A Kinnane (52'), (62'), (65'), A Down (84')

10/04/22 - Aylesford Ladies 1-10 Ashford Town (Middlesex) FC Women

Lineup - S Shults, A Kinnane, C Baker, E Clarabut, H Pearson, J Hoesli-Atkins, A Down (captain), K Peart, J Johnson, A Cheatley, L Neufville

Scorers - A Cheatley (2'), (6') (70'), L Neufville (4'), (20'), (30'), A Kinnane (60'), (73'), H Pearson (66'), A Down (90+3')

24/04/22 - Fulham Women 0-1 Ashford Town (Middlesex) FC Women

Lineup - S Shults, A Kinnane, E Clarabut, H Pearson, J Hoesli-Atkins, A Down (captain), K Peart, J Johnson, R Linton, A Cheatley, L Neufville

Scorers - L Neufville (60')

01/05/22 - Ashford Town (Middlesex) FC Women 4-1 Whyteleafe

Lineup - S Shults, L Huse, C Baker, H Pearson, C Farrell, A Down (captain), K Peart, J Johnson, R Linton, A Cheatley, L Neufville

Scorers - R Linton (25'), A Cheatley (35'), L Neufville (65'), (84')

Hello Women's National League.

We pulled off arguably the result of the round in The Vitality Women's FA Cup by defeating FAWNL Southern Premier side Oxford United 3-0. They were three leagues above, this is a game I can never forget.

Chris Benn / Flickr

**Middlesex FA Girls' Centre of Excellence Belgium Tour 2015.
Coaching for the centre gave me an unrivalled experience at the
elite level of the game.**
Middlesex CofE

The most successful captain in the clubs history. They just
don't make them like this anymore.
Neil Cole

This image of me embracing Jordanne Hoesli-Atkins after our cup victory epitomizes how I feel about each of the individuals at this football club. We're one big tangerine family. Perfectly imperfect.

Neil Cole

PLAYERS UNDER MY MANAGEMENT

Below are the list of players I had the pleasure in coaching at the football club. The range of emotions you go through as a coach is unparalleled, no matter the level you compete at, no matter the sport. One thing I would never change are the players that I had under my guardship - they all played a hand in shaping this football club. Every single player has contributed - I will forever be grateful for the role everyone has played.

1. Sophie Shults
2. Gracie Perkis
3. Sophie Burgess
4. Lauren Restel
5. Nicole Jacobs
6. Mara DeLuca
7. Millie Maggionni
8. Jaime Gotch
9. Jade Harker
10. Nadia Peters

11. Ashleigh Harte
12. Alice Frice
13. Drew Lawrence
14. Alex Beauchamp
15. Katie Gavin
16. Jemma Berggren
17. Sasha Treadaway
18. Maddie Bone
19. Tara Mills
20. Beth Sheehan
21. Jessica Boyd
22. Harriet Freeman
23. Amber Luzar
24. Judith Densu
25. Paige Pantlin
26. Ella Dodd
27. Charlotte McGregor
28. Frida Larsson
29. Tia Prior
30. Anya Kinnane
31. Ellen Clarabut
32. Laura Huse
33. Hannah Pearson
34. Charlotte Baker
35. France Cotter
36. Jordanne Hoesli-Atkins
37. Emily Reynolds
38. Samara Phillips-Hines
39. Alice Down
40. Chloe Farrell

41. Vicky James
42. Holly Symons
43. Kalani Peart
44. Stephanie Mann
45. Carla Novakovic
46. Elizabeth Kriebel
47. Gemma Goodwin
48. Holly Reid
49. Lauren Richardson
50. Latoya Bailey
51. Chloe Dalrymple
52. Hannah Noonan
53. Kodi Spencer
54. Megan McGarvey
55. Jade Johnson
56. Ella Hill
57. Rebecca French
58. Ellie Butcher
59. Rebecca Thurlow
60. Rozalia Sitarz
61. Lucy Potter
62. Claire Samuels
63. Geraldine Burgess
64. Irisha Smith
65. Charmaine Benham
66. Milly Adcock
67. Holly Isaacs
68. Ruby Linton
69. Amy Holdcroft
70. Ashley Cheatley

71. Lavana Neufville
72. Bahra Keeping
73. Phoebe Head
74. Hannah Nebbitt
75. Jo Wilson
76. Sofia Carpenter
77. Rebecca Fisher
78. Elin Jones
79. Gemma Cottrell
80. Katie Williams
81. Lucy Thornton
82. Caroline Bisson
83. Sequoia Belworthy
84. Dana Johnson
85. Nicole Douglas
86. Hannah Quinton
87. Tilly Frost
88. Amy O'Sullivan
89. Lucy Easton

Thank you Tangerines. We are National.

Lightning Source UK Ltd.
Milton Keynes UK
UKHW020649290622
405123UK00009B/676